The Philosophy Skills Book

Exercises in Critical Reading, Writing and Thinking

Stephen J. Finn, Chris Case,
Bob Underwood and Jesse Zuck

D0869983

BLOOMSBURY

LONDON • NEW DELHI • NEW YORK • SYDNEY

Bloomsbury Academic

An imprint of Bloomsbury Publishing Plc

50 Bedford Square 175 Fifth Avenue
London New York
WC1B 3DP NY 10010
UK USA

www.bloomsbury.com

First published in 2012 by the Continuum International Publishing Group Ltd
Reprinted by Bloomsbury Academic 2013

British Library Cataloguing-in-Publication Data
A catalogue record for this book is available from the British Library.

ISBN: HB: 978-1-4411-9874-7
PB: 978-1-4411-2456-2

Library of Congress Cataloging-in-Publication Data
The philosophy skills book: exercises in critical reading, writing, and
thinking/Stephen J. Finn . . . [et al.].
p. cm.
Includes bibliographical references (p.).
ISBN 978-1-4411-9874-7 (hardcover) – ISBN 978-1-4411-2456-2 (pbk.)
– ISBN 978-1-4411-6742-2 (ebook (pdf)) – ISBN 978-1-4411-2385-5
(ebook (epub)) 1. Philosophy–Textbooks. I. Finn, Stephen J. II. Title.
BD31.P57 2012
107.1–dc23
2011034919

Typeset by Newgen Imaging Systems Pvt Ltd, Chennai, India
Printed and bound in Great Britain

The Philosophy Skills Book

Online resources to accompany this book are available online at: http://www.bloomsbury.com/uk/the-philosophy-skills-book-9781441124562/

Please visit the link to access these downloadable resources.

If you experience any problems accessing the resources, please contact Bloomsbury at: companionwebsites@bloomsbury.com

Also available from Bloomsbury

A to Z Philosophy, Alexander Moseley
Doing Philosophy, Clare Saunders, Danielle Lamb, David Mossley
and George MacDonald Ross

Contents

Introduction

Why use this book?

There are many possible ways to approach the study of philosophy, which can be a difficult subject to learn. The task of grasping its technical terminology, its abstract subject matter and its seemingly complex procedures can appear daunting to a student approaching philosophy for the first time. Philosophy is composed of not only a large body of accumulated knowledge, but also, as an academic discipline, it has developed a set of tools for dealing with this knowledge in order to make sense of it. One approach to philosophy is to take an historical tack by working one's way chronologically through the writings of important philosophers. While the historical approach has its merits, we feel that it needs to be supplemented by an approach that views philosophy as an activity and not just as a study of a body of knowledge. A helpful distinction to make is the one between studying philosophical ideas and doing philosophy. Our goal is to help students learn to do philosophy, not just to become acquainted with philosophical ideas. Thus, the book is designed to help develop the skills required to analyze and evaluate philosophical concepts, arguments and theories.

How to use this book: Students

This book is targeted at students enrolled in introductory philosophy courses. It is intended to be an exercise book that helps you hone skills necessary for success in such a course. The exercises in the book are *mostly* independent of each other, such that you do not need to work through the exercises in the order presented. However, we have sequenced them in a useful order so that they build upon each other in developing important skills.

Furthermore, the chapters are very short and we try to focus on what we consider the most critical aspects of the skill under discussion. We have decided to take this approach for two reasons. First, we recognize that this book will likely be used as a supplement to other texts in your course. Thus, we do not want to burden you with a great deal of additional reading, but want to encourage you to spend a considerable amount of time on the exercises themselves. Second, we hope that much of the information provided in the chapters will be covered in more detail in other places, such as in your main textbook or in your classroom sessions. The unique nature of this book consists in the fact that it is primarily an exercise book that gets you to practice philosophical skills rather than a textbook that focuses on conveying an extensive amount of philosophical content.

We have provided answers to some of the exercises, but not all. We would like to stress, however, that our answers are precisely that, that is, *our* answers. While many of the questions in this book have 'objective' answers, a large number of them require interpretation of philosophical texts and ideas; as such, some questions involve more subjective elements. By not including answers to all questions, we want to put some of the responsibility on you to answer these questions for yourself. Please keep in mind, then, that your answers may well differ from ours. While we believe that some answers or responses are better and more reasonable than others, an important part of doing philosophy is the recognition that one has license to answer philosophical questions on one's own. Do not mistake this license, however, for the freedom to answer in any way that you want; you have the responsibility to defend your answers through rational argumentation. Furthermore, for many of these exercises, we cannot know in advance your answers and the reasons you might have to support them. Therefore, we suggest that you answer all the questions on your own, before looking at any of the answers we provide.

Even though these exercises may be done individually or in groups, we believe a dialectical approach is extremely helpful. We suggest, in other words, that you work on these exercises with others or, at the least, that you share your answers with others and compare and contrast your answers. In short, the exercises are a good way to 'do philosophy' with others.

How to use this book: Teachers

While we hope that teachers will find all of the exercises useful and relevant, we recognize that such hope may be forlorn. Philosophy teachers are usually very particular about their own views of what counts as doing philosophy and what counts as doing it well. Nevertheless, we have designed the exercises so that a good handful of them should be useful in any introductory philosophy course, whatever approach an instructor adopts.

We recommend that teachers pick and choose the exercises that are relevant to their concerns and pedagogical methods. Also, we recommend that instructors use the exercises in a variety of different ways. For some of the shorter exercises, for example, instructors might employ them as in-class exercises for both individual and group work. On the other hand, the more time-consuming questions might be used as homework assignments. Instructors may also try a hybrid approach that involves having students work on the assignments outside of class on their own, but then have students discuss their answers in class. Whether the exercises should be used as in-class, out-of-class, group or individual assignments is completely at the instructor's discretion.

In an effort to make this task of choosing appropriate exercises easy, we have included two matrices to help you identify exercises according to topic or author, respectively. Throughout the book, students will be asked to focus their attention on short (and sometimes long) passages from primary philosophical texts. We have classified most of these passages into one of the five major branches of philosophy: metaphysics, epistemology, ethics, political philosophy and philosophy of religion. Thus, if you are teaching a course thematically, you can pick passages that address the particular branch of philosophy you are currently covering. Similarly, if your students are reading a particular philosopher, you might choose an exercise that is based on a passage from that philosopher. In any case, the matrices are found directly after this introduction. We hope that you will find your own unique ways of using these exercises to best help your students become better readers, better thinkers and better philosophers.

The format of the book is basically the same throughout, that is, each chapter contains a short discussion about a particular philosophical skill followed by an exercise or series of exercises. While many of the exercises could probably be done without reading the introductory material in the chapter itself, we strongly recommend that you assign the chapter as a whole or else cover the main ideas in class before having your students do the exercises. We have kept the chapters short so that your students can spend most of their time on the exercises.

Disclaimer

It is important to be clear about what this book is not. It is not a work of philosophy. It is a work primarily about how to do philosophy. Any assertions or claims in the book that are, or appear to be, contentious, unsupported by argument, etc., are that way because we neither had the space to adequately defend them, nor did we find such defence suitable for an introductory text. As philosophy instructors ourselves, we sometimes complain about the lack of precision in introductory textbooks. We fully recognize that numerous claims made in the chapters are neither completely accurate nor fully developed. You may find, for example, that you or your philosophy instructor disagrees with some of our assertions, which may be about specific philosophical ideas or about methods for doing philosophy. We do not see this as a problem, but as an opportunity for you (and your instructor) to explore the ideas further. If this disclaimer seems unimportant at first, once you start doing philosophy you will understand why such a disclaimer becomes necessary.

Topic Matrix

Topic	
Metaphysics	Ch. 1, Part B, Passage 3
	Ch. 2, Part B, Passages 2, 4, 5
	Ch. 6, all passages
	Ch. 11, Passages 1, 5
	Ch. 13, Passages 1, 5
	Ch. 24, Passage 2

Epistemology	Ch. 2, Part B, Passage 1
	Ch. 19, Passage 7
	Ch. 24, Passage 1
Ethics	Ch. 2, Part B, Passages3, 4
	Ch. 3, Part B, Passage 1
	Ch. 11, Passages 2, 4
	Ch. 13, Passage 4
	Ch. 17, Passages 1, 4
	Ch. 19, Passage 8
	Ch. 26, Passage 1
Political philosophy	Ch. 1, Part B, Passages 1, 2
	Ch. 11, Passage 4
	Ch. 13, Passage 2
	Ch. 17, Passages 2, 3, 5
	Ch. 19, Passage 6
	Ch. 20, Passage 1
	Ch. 23, Passage 1
	Ch. 24, Passage 3
	Ch. 25, Passage 1
	Ch. 26, Passage 2
Philosophy of religion	Ch. 11, Passage 3
	Ch. 17, Passage 6
	Ch. 19, Passages 9, 10
	Ch. 24, Passage 5

Author Matrix

This list does not include all references to every author, only to the passages of significant length and philosophical content.

Antiphon	Ch. 24, Passage 3
Aristotle	Ch.17, Passage 1
Albert Camus	Ch. 2, Passage 4
René Descartes	Ch. 6, Passage 2
	Ch. 19, Passage 9
Gay-Williams	Ch. 25, Passage 1
John Hick	Ch. 19, Passage 10

Martin Heidegger	Ch. 13, Passage 5
Thomas Hobbes	Ch. 20, Passage 1
	Ch. 24, Passage 2
David Hume	Ch. 17, Passage 6
	Ch. 24, Passage 1
Immanuel Kant	Ch. 19, Passage 8
	Ch. 24, Passage 4
John Locke	Ch. 11, Passage 1
J. L. Mackie	Ch. 24, Passage 5
Niccolò Machiavelli	Ch. 13, Passage 2
J. S. Mill	Ch. 17, Passage 4
Friedrich Nietzsche	Ch. 13, Passage 3
Robert Nozick	Ch. 11, Passage 2
	Ch. 17, Passage 3
Blaise Pascal	Ch. 11, Passage 3
C. S. Peirce	Ch. 2, Passage 1
Karl Popper	Ch. 19, Passage 7
Plato	Ch. 3, Part B, Passage 1
	Ch. 13, Passage 1
John Perry	Ch. 11, Passage 5
James Rachels	Ch. 2, Passage 3
Richard Rorty	Ch. 26, Passage 2
Jean-Jacques Rousseau	Ch. 19, Passage 6
Gilbert Ryle	Ch. 2, Passage 3
Jean Paul Sartre	Ch. 13, Passage 4
J. F. Stephen	Ch. 17, Passage 2
Richard Taylor	Ch. 2, Passage 3
Judith Jarvis Thomson	Ch. 11, Passage 4
	Ch. 26, Passage 1
Ernest van den Haag	Ch. 23, Passage 1
Michael Walzer	Ch. 17, Passage 5

Note on the text

You can find answers at the end of the book to questions marked with an *.

1 Raising philosophical questions

A novice to philosophical inquiry must first acquire the ability to recognize and to raise philosophical questions. While you have undoubtedly asked many philosophical questions in your life (such questions as: 'Why do I exist?', 'What is the purpose of human life?', 'Does God exist?', 'Is capital punishment wrong?'), this may be the first time that you are expected to raise, and attempt to answer, philosophical questions in a systematic fashion. But what exactly is a philosophical question? What sets philosophy apart from other disciplines? As you might expect, even philosophers themselves disagree about the specific content, goals and methods of philosophical questioning. Nevertheless, we suspect that most philosophers would agree with the following two claims:

1. Philosophers raise questions about *fundamental matters*.
2. Philosophical questions are often *open ended* because their answers are not attained by empirical observation alone.

When we say philosophers raise *open-ended* questions concerning *fundamental matters*, we mean that they seek basic and underlying principles of reality and life that are not simply obtained by empirical observation. An astrophysicist might ask, for example, the following question: 'When and how did the universe form?' Yet, a philosopher would ask a deeper question: 'Why is there a universe at all?' Similarly, while a neuroscientist might be interested in knowing what neurons fire when a human being makes a decision, a philosopher seeks to discover whether we are free to make decisions at all. In both of these cases, the answer to a non-philosophical question is *factual*, that is, it is theoretically capable of being attained through empirical research, whereas the answer to the philosophical question is not. The initial step to thinking like a philosopher, then, is learning to see that a philosophical question is lurking about in a common event or activity. In daily life, we often encounter opportunities for entering into philosophical discussion, yet we ignore such opportunities. For example, assume a town council has just passed a new law requiring all bicycle riders to wear helmets. You might wonder about the role of town government in regulating your decisions and thereby raise such philosophical questions as: 'What gives the town government the right to regulate my personal actions?', 'Why should I obey a law I disagree with?', 'Who has the right to determine what is best for me and for society in general?'

Exercises

Part A
Instructions
Classify each of the following questions as philosophical (P) or non-philosophical (NP) and explain your reasoning for the classification.

   *1. Is smoking dangerous to your physical health?
   2. Is it right for basketball players to cheat?
   3. Is technology necessary for human life to be fulfilling?
   4. How many lives could be saved if we outlawed smoking?
   *5. How does the human brain process new information?
   6. Is it the role of government to protect its citizens from themselves?
   7. Are humans free to pursue their own interests?
   8. What concrete benefits arise from multitasking?
   *9. Is death necessarily bad?
   10. What are the emotional effects of stress in humans?

Part B
Instructions
Imagine you have the opportunity to ask one philosophical question to the authors of each of the passages below. What would you ask?

*Passage 1

In any event, the reason that the NCAA [National Collegiate Athletic Association in the United States] should welcome legal gambling on its games is that the casinos in Las Vegas, with a major vested interest in the games being played above board, are motivated to monitor the betting action on any games. When the action deviates from normal expectations, as it did with a number of games played by the Arizona State University basketball team in 1994, the casinos will alert the FBI. In the Arizona State case, a subsequent FBI investigation uncovered point-shaving by a number of basketball players. In effect, legal gambling and law enforcement can work hand in glove. Illegal bookmakers are not likely to be motivated to police the integrity of the game for the general public's edification. Were they to do so by involving law enforcement agencies, they would expose themselves to penalties for illegal bookmaking. Their only way of handling losses incurred by point-shaving and the throwing of games where they were not the instigators of the players' behavior might be the breaking of the bodily parts of the offending players or worse.[1]

Passage 2

One in four Americans can expect to contract cancer during his or her lifetime. The American Cancer Society estimated that 420,000 Americans would die of cancer in 1981. The Society's estimate for 2002 is 555,500 deaths from cancer, with almost 1.3 million new cases diagnosed that year. "A 1978 report issued by the President's Council on Environmental Quality (CEQ) unequivocally states that 'most researchers agree that 70 to 90 per cent of cancers are caused by environmental influences and hence theoretically preventable.'" This means that a concerted national effort could result in saving 350,000 or more lives a year and reducing each individual's chances of getting cancer in his or her lifetime from 1 in 4 to 1 in 12 or fewer. If you think this would require a massive effort in terms of money and personnel, you are right. How much of an effort, though, would the nation make to stop a foreign invader who was killing a thousand people a day and bent on slaughtering one-quarter of the present population? . . . In the face of this 'invasion' that is already under way, the U.S. Government allocated $1.9 billion to the National Cancer Institute (NCI) for fiscal year 1992, and NCI allocated $219 million to the study of the physical and chemical (i.e., environmental) causes of cancer. Compare this with the (at least) $45 billion spent at the time to fight the 1991 Persian Gulf war. The simple truth is that the government that strove so mightily to protect the borders of a small, undemocratic nation 7,000 miles away is doing next to nothing to protect us against the chemical war in our midst.[2]

Passage 3

Just how adaptable are humans? That is the question underlying pervasive worries about the impact of modern technology, especially the boom in the use of personal laptops and hand-held devices, like the iPad and smartphones. Are we becoming skilled multitaskers? Or are we sacrificing our attention to long-term goals for the more primitive gratification of skimming tweets and e-mail messages? There are indeed some gloomy answers to these questions . . . But we think there's a flip side to the story of technological harm. In fact, the story may be mostly flip side. Some statistics show a three-fold increase in the consumption of 'media' between 1996 and 2008. It's hard to be happy if that means mostly watching 'Lost' on a miniature screen. But 'media' in this sense means everything that flows through your desktop, laptop or smartphone. It has an addictive quality, in part because it reinforces deeply human traits – above all, a desire for social connection and mental stimulus. The electronic informational environment we live in is hardly passive. It is responsive, playful, and – yes – sometimes inane and trivial, not unlike our social discourse in the real world, including the world of families. Yet when have humans ever had more immediate access to solid information? The Web may be a whirlpool of myth and misinformation, but it has also become a global library of fact and data. How we use it to enrich our lives – including our social lives – is an ongoing experiment in adaptation . . . Like most technologies, our new electronic digisphere is made up of good and bad. How we use it is, as always, up to us.[3]

2 Active reading skills

Philosophy reading assignments can seem impenetrable to many students. You should be aware that such reading assignments will likely come in a variety of forms: primary texts, textbooks, anthologies, secondary sources, among others. *Primary texts*, which can be the most challenging to read, refer to the original works of philosophy written by philosophers themselves. Philosophy *textbooks*, which often include numerous excerpts from primary texts, offer a general introduction to important philosophers and their ideas. Philosophical *anthologies* often have long excerpts (if not complete works) of primary texts accompanied by very short introductions or overviews. *Secondary sources*, which provide interpretations, critical evaluations or detailed analyses of primary texts, are a good source of information about philosophy. When reading philosophical texts, especially primary sources, there are a number of reasons why the texts may appear impenetrable. The abstract nature of philosophical ideas, the natural ambiguity of certain words, novel or idiosyncratic uses of terms, problems of translation, poor expression on the part of the author, an historical gap between writer and reader are among these reasons. Often, you must spend a lot of time and energy to simply understand what the philosopher is saying in the reading before you can judge the merit of the ideas in play.

In this chapter, we introduce you to a common reading strategy, referred to as SQ3R, a strategy especially helpful for reading philosophy. SQ3R stands for: *Survey, Question, Read, Recall, Review.*[1]

1. *Survey*: In the first step of this reading strategy, you survey the reading assignment in an effort to get the 'big picture', that is, get a sense of the main ideas that will be covered

in the text. In this step, pay special attention to the text's overall organization, to the reading's titles and subtitles, to accentuated words or phrases and to graphics.

2. *Question*: Before reading the assignment, give yourself a purpose by raising a number of questions about the reading assignment. An easy way to do this is to change the titles, subtitles, bold-faced words, etc., into questions. For example, if the title of a section in the book is '*Cogito Ergo Sum*', convert it into the question 'What does "*cogito ergo sum*" mean?' Furthermore, the following questions usually help you find a purpose in reading philosophy:
   a. Who is the author and why did she write this?
   b. What is the author's primary claim?
   c. What arguments or evidence are provided to support the claims?
   d. Is there information peripheral to the main claim?
   e. Do I agree with the author? Why or why not?

3. *Read*: When reading the assignment, take an active approach. Try not to worry about the resale value of your text (assuming, of course, that you are not borrowing one from the library) and actively mark it up by underlining main ideas, circling unknown words, placing question marks near confusing passages and bracketing passages that do not seem essential to the main points. Annotate the text by paraphrasing and condensing the main ideas in the margins. Also, use the margins to react to the text, briefly noting your own thoughts and possible objections.

4. *Recall*: Write a summary, in your own words, of the main ideas. Write out your answers to the questions raised in Step 2.

5. *Review*: Before class, review your summary, the text and your annotations.

Exercise

*Part A
Instructions
Choose any chapter from a philosophical text that you own and answer the following questions:

1. What is the title of the chapter, and how does it fit into the overall organization of the book?
2. Does the chapter title reveal anything to you about its content? If so, what?
3. What are the subtitles and section headings? What, if anything, do these reveal about the content of the chapter? Also, based on the title, is there anything that is completely unknown to you?
4. Are there any accentuated words or passages (boldfaced, italicized, highlighted)?

Part B

Instructions

For each of the passages below, do the following:

1. Underline sentences or phrases that you believe express the main ideas of the passage.
2. Circle unknown words.
3. Place question marks near confusing passages.
4. Bracket passages, if any, that do not seem essential to the main point or that merely restate or elaborate upon one of the main ideas.
5. For the passage, summarize main points in your own words in the margin.
6. Raise one objection and write it in the margin.
7. If possible, compare your answers with others.

---

*Passage 1

One theory of truth is the *pragmatic* theory. Pragmatism, a native American philosophical school which began with the work of Charles Sanders Peirce in the nineteenth century, emphasizes the close relationship between thinking and acting. Indeed, thinking is viewed by the pragmatists as a problem-solving activity. Ideas are plans of action; the meaning of ideas or terms is reducible to their concrete, practical implications. On the subject of truth, pragmatists tell us that a statement is true if, when we act upon it, we actually encounter the consequences which the statement implies, anticipates, or predicts. Every meaning-ful statement, they argue, can be translated into a set of con-sequences which is supposed to follow if specific operations are performed. So perform the operations, and observe whether the consequences ensue. If so, the statement is true; if not, it is false. For instance, let us suppose that your doctor diagnoses an ailment of yours as an allergy to chlorine, which you encoun-ter frequently since swimming is one of your hobbies. Is his or her diagnosis, formulated in the statement, 'You are allergic to chlorine', true or false? This statement implies that you should stop swimming and exposing yourself to chlorine for a time, then the ailment will disappear. If you do the former, and the latter ensues, a pragmatist would say that the doctor's statement is true; if the ailment continues, however, the diagnosis would be false.[2]

Passage 2

We are all, at certain moments of pain, threat, or bereavement, apt to entertain the idea of fatalism, the thought that what is hap-pening at a particular moment is unavoidable, that we are power-less to prevent it. Sometimes we find ourselves in circumstances not of our own making, in which our very being and destinies are so thoroughly anchored that the thought of fatalism can be quite overwhelming, and sometimes consoling. One feels that whatever then happens, however good or ill, will be what those circumstances yield, and we are helpless. Soldiers, it is said, are sometimes possessed by such thoughts. Perhaps everyone would feel more inclined to them if they paused once in a while to think of how little they ever had to do with bringing themselves to wherever they had arrived in life, how much of their fortunes and destinies were decided for them by sheer circumstance, and how the entire course of their lives is often set, once and for all, by the most trivial incidents, which they did not produce and could not have foreseen. If we are free to work on our destinies at all, which is doubtful, we have freedom that is at best exercised within exceedingly narrow paths. All the important things – when we are born, of what parents, into what culture, whether we are

loved or rejected, whether we are male or female, our temperament, our intelligence or stupidity, indeed everything that makes
for the bulk of our happiness and misery – all these are decided
for us by the most casual and indifferent circumstances, by sheer
coincidences, chance encounters, and seemingly insignificant
fortuities.[3]

Passage 3

To many thinkers, this observation – 'Different cultures have different moral codes' – has seemed to be the key to understanding
morality. The idea of universal truth in ethics, they say, is a myth.
The customs of different societies are all that exists. These customs cannot be said to be 'correct' or 'incorrect', for that implies
we have an independent standard of right and wrong by which
they may be judged. But there is no such independent standard;
every standard is culture-bound . . . This line of thought has probably persuaded more people to be skeptical about ethics than
any other single thing. Cultural Relativism as it has been called,
challenges our ordinary belief in the objectivity and universality
of moral truth. It says, in effect, that there is no such thing as
universal truth in ethics; there are only the various cultural codes,
and nothing more.[4]

[handwritten margin notes: "There is something as right and wrong" and "I believe there is a standard as right and wrong even when wrong according to others. Universal"]

Passage 4

There is but one truly serious philosophical problem, and that is
suicide. Judging whether life is or is not worth living amounts to
answering the fundamental question of philosophy. All the rest –
whether or not the world has three dimensions, whether the
mind has nine or twelve categories – comes afterwards. These
are games; one must first answer. And if it is true, as Nietzsche
claims, that a philosopher, to deserve our respect, must preach
by example, you can appreciate the importance of that reply, for
it will precede the definitive act. These are facts the heart can
feel; yet they call for careful study before they become clear to
the intellect.

If I ask myself how to judge that this question is more urgent than that, I reply that one judges by the actions it entails. I have never seen anyone die for the ontological argument. Galileo, who held a scientific truth of great importance, abjured it with the greatest ease as soon as it endangered his life. In a certain sense, he did right. That truth was not worth the stake. Whether the earth or the sun revolves around the others is a matter of profound indifference. To tell the truth, it is a futile question. On the other hand, I see many people die because they judge this life is not worth living. I see others paradoxically getting killed for the ideas or illusions that give them a reason for living (what is called a reason for living is also an excellent reason for dying). I therefore conclude that the meaning of life is the most urgent of questions.[5]

Passage 5

A word about what is meant by the term 'Mind' (manas) in Buddhist philosophy may be useful here. It should be very clearly understood that mind is not spirit as opposed to matter. It should always be remembered that Buddhism does not recognize a spirit opposed to matter, as is accepted by most other systems of philosophies and religions. Mind is only a faculty or organ (indriya) like the eye or the ear. It can be controlled and developed like any other faculty, and the Buddha speaks quite often of the value of controlling and disciplining these six faculties. The difference between the eye and the mind as faculties is that the former senses the world of colours and visible forms, while the latter senses the world of ideas and thoughts and mental objects. We cannot hear colours, but we can see them. Nor can we see sounds, but we can hear them, thus with our five physical sense-organs – eye, ear, nose, tongue, body – we experience only the world of visible forms, sounds, odours, tastes, and tangible objects. What of ideas and thoughts? They are also a part of the world. But they cannot be sensed, they cannot be conceived by the faculty of the eye, ear, nose, tongue or body. Yet they can be conceived by another faculty, which is mind. Now ideas and thoughts are not independent of the world experienced by these five physical sense faculties. In fact they depend on, and are conditioned by, physical experiences. Hence a person born blind cannot have ideas of colour, except through analogy of sounds or some other things experienced through his other faculties. Ideas and thoughts which form a part of the world are thus produced and conditioned by physical experiences and are conceived by the mind. Hence mind (*manas*) is considered a sense faculty or organ (*indriya*), like the eye or the ear.[6]

3 Getting the most out of class

Although we often wish that students were enrolled in introductory philosophy courses out of a specific desire to study our discipline, we recognize that many students are required to study philosophy to satisfy a general educational requirement. If your philosophy course is mandatory, you may not always be motivated to study philosophy for its own sake. We encourage you, however, to try to take full advantage of your access to a philosophical expert, who is ready and willing to share her knowledge, and to a group of individuals (i.e., fellow students) who are likely encountering philosophical ideas in a systematic fashion for the first time. One of the best ways to take advantage of these two resources is to get the most out of each class session. The benefits of the class time itself, however, depend upon what you do before, during and after each class session. The following suggestions are aimed to help you get the most out of class.

Before class

- Read the assigned reading (using the active techniques discussed in Chapter 2).
- Write down questions concerning the reading and the previous class session and raise these questions in class.
- Spend a few minutes thinking about your own ideas on the topic. What is your opinion and what good reasons do you have for holding it?
- Review your class notes from the previous session.

During class

- Take notes (see suggestions below).
- Ask questions whenever you are confused.
- Challenge, politely and reasonably, the expressed opinions of your instructor and fellow students.
- Stay engaged during discussion periods with fellow students.

After class

- Review your notes from the class session and note any problems/confusion.
- Ask the instructor for help clarifying the problematic issues.
- Reconsider your opinions on the topic. Did your opinions change? Why or why not?
- If walking to another class with a student, why not continue the discussion and talk about the most interesting ideas covered?

An important method for using class time wisely is taking good notes. Research strongly suggests that students who actively take notes in class perform better on tests, write stronger papers and retain more information. Here is a list of recommended strategies.[1]

- Write notes legibly and clearly. There is no reason to cram your notes, but it is helpful to leave space in the margins for making corrections or for summarizing main ideas later. *Common sense*
- When there is a pause in the lecture, review the most recent notes to ensure they are clear. Make corrections as needed. *Good Advice*
- Make sure to highlight, underline or circle main ideas and concepts. Use margins to highlight or summarize key concepts.
- Pay attention to your instructor's behaviour, since certain types of behaviour signal important ideas. For example, watch for such things as intentional repetition, pauses, a change in pace, a deepening of tone, use of the blackboard or use of slides. *Very interesting never thought of that before*

- If possible, try to arrange the information into a concept map, diagram or picture.
- Create and use your own method for shorthand. For example, you might use w/o for 'without'.
- Choose appropriate times to take notes and take notes quickly. If the instructor begins to repeat a point you have already grasped, for example, use the time to take notes or review your most recent notes.
- If the instructor is speaking too quickly or has moved on to a new point before you have fully grasped the previous point, don't be afraid to politely ask the instructor to slow down.
- Leave blank areas for parts of a lecture in which you have lost concentration and then, with the help of the instructor or a classmate, fill in the space at a later time.
- Use the margins to make your own comments and observations on the notes.
- Within 24 hours, go back over your notes to see if there are ways to improve them. Spend a few minutes to revise or edit them, or to write questions to pursue with your instructor or a classmate.

It is important to add a qualification to the importance of note taking. You don't need to be a court stenographer in class who captures every word that is said. There is a difference between collecting data and actively participating in class. If you spend too much time in class collecting data, you may miss out on figuring out how to understand it later. There is no need to capture everything said in the classroom, especially if it takes away from the time in class that should be used for thinking about the material.

One last tip for getting the most out of class is figuring out why a particular class session matters to the course as a whole. In most courses, philosophy instructors will design their courses in blocks of material, so that many class sessions are connected in an important way. Thus, at the end of each session, you might ask yourself: 'What is the point of the material?', 'How does it fit with other material in the course?', 'What is the goal of learning it?' If you cannot answer these questions yourself, you should ask your instructor for assistance. Being clear on the 'so what' for each class can help with your overall understanding and with your ability to do philosophy.

Exercise

Part A
Instructions
Before your next class, share our suggestions for note taking with a classmate. After your next class session, use the suggestions for note taking provided in the chapter and compare and contrast your notes with your classmate's notes. What did you see as the main topics? Did your partner have a similar view of the main ideas? Did you both organize your notes in the same way? If not, which way seemed to be more effective? Why is this material important to the course? How is it related to the topic from the previous class session?

Part B
Instructions
Read the following passage from Plato's *Euthyphro* as if it were assigned in your course. Write down questions concerning the reading that you would raise in class. Spend a few minutes thinking about your own opinions on the topic. What is your position, and what good reasons do you have for holding it?

Passage

SOCRATES: The point which I should first wish to understand is whether the pious or holy is beloved by the gods because it is holy, or holy because it is beloved of the gods . . . [so] what do you say of piety, Euthyphro: is not piety . . . loved by all the gods?

EUTHYPHRO: Yes.

SOCRATES: Because it is pious or holy, or for some other reason?

EUTHYPHRO: No, that is the reason.

SOCRATES: It is loved because it is holy, not holy because it is loved?

EUTHYPHRO: Yes.

SOCRATES: And that which is dear to the gods is loved by them, and is in a state to be loved of them because it is loved of them?

EUTHYPHRO: Certainly.

SOCRATES: Then that which is dear to the gods, Euthyphro, is not holy, nor is that which is holy loved of God, as you affirm; but they are two different things.

EUTHYPHRO: How do you mean, Socrates?

SOCRATES: I mean to say that the holy has been acknowledged by us to be loved of God because it is holy, not to be holy because it is loved.

EUTHYPHRO: Yes.

SOCRATES: But that which is dear to the gods is dear to them because it is loved by them, not loved by them because it is dear to them.

EUTHYPHRO: True.

SOCRATES: But, friend Euthyphro, if that which is holy is the same with that which is dear to God, and is loved because it is holy, then that which is dear to God would have been loved as being dear to God; but if that which is dear to God is dear to him because loved by him, then that which is holy would have been holy because loved by him . . . Thus you appear to me, Euthyphro, when I ask you what is the essence of holiness, to offer an attribute only, and not the essence – the attribute of being loved by all the gods. But you still refuse to explain to me the nature of holiness . . .

EUTHYPHRO: I really do not know, Socrates, how to express what I mean. For somehow or other our arguments, on whatever ground we rest them, seem to turn round and walk away from us.[2]

Part C

Instructions

This exercise is a group activity that requires two people. Have one person read the following teacher–student exchange, while the other takes notes and develops a follow-up question. Then, switch roles and compare notes and questions.

Student–teacher dialogue

Teacher: Last night you read about the 'Euthyphro problem'. Socrates says to Euthyphro, 'Thus you appear to me, Euthyphro, when I ask you what is the essence of holiness, to offer an attribute only, and not the essence.' Here Socrates has put the fine point on his argument about holiness. This is the real upshot of asking 'whether the pious or holy is beloved by the gods because it is holy, or holy because it is beloved of the gods'. Socrates is trying to force Euthyphro to give an account that he finds most interesting and most needed: an account that provides the intrinsic nature of piety or holiness. Although you did not read the end of the dialogue, it ends with Euthyphro throwing his hands up in frustration. It is a frustration that we can feel as well, for as soon as you understand the question Socrates is asking – is it holy because God loves it, or is it holy in its own right – you begin to get a sense for the stakes involved in the answer.

It is important here to note a few things. First, this is a metaphysical question that Socrates asks. He is after the essential property or properties of holiness. That is, the thing or group of things that 'holiness' and only 'holiness' has. Certainly, there can be many things that are loved by gods – fame, revenge, intrigue – but, none of these are thereby holy. What Socrates is after, and what we hope to find as well, is the essence of holiness. What is it that can justify the use of the term and what we do in service of it?

Second, Socrates is also raising the question about the relationship of ethics and religion. More specifically, he is asking whether the gods are responsible for creating morality or whether gods are constrained by morality. In other words, is something wrong because the gods say it is or do they say it is wrong because it is? If you think an act is wrong because God says it is, then you would accept the 'divine command theory', which is the view that God creates moral rules. If you think God says something is wrong because it is wrong, then you probably think that moral rules are above God. God, in other words, knows that something is wrong and that is why He forbids it.

Third, the Euthyphro problem does not go away when we turn our attention away from holiness and the gods. It is a problem that applies more generally to almost any moral or normative concept you might offer up. When we go searching for the properties of 'goodness', or 'justice', we can always ask the question to ourselves: 'Do I find this to be good because it is good, or is it simply something that has become dear to me?'

So, what do you think about the Euthyphro problem? Any questions?

Student: Don't we need God to have morality?

Teacher: Why do you think that?

Student: Because without God, what would prevent people from doing whatever they wanted?

Teacher: The laws, perhaps? Do you think you behave appropriately because there is a God? Don't you just think you do the right thing because it is right?

Student: I think most people would behave immorally if there was no God and they thought they could get away with it.

4 Philosophical discussion

Socrates, one of the most important philosophers in the history of Western thought, is known for using discussion as the primary means for philosophical investigation. Although writing is now the dominant form of exchanging philosophical ideas, the ability to discuss is still important for philosophical discovery and argumentation. One of our fundamental beliefs is that philosophy is not simply an intellectual exercise, but a life-transforming activity. As such, we view philosophical discussion with others as an integral part of philosophy. In your philosophy course, we hope that you will have the opportunity to discuss ideas with both your fellow students and your instructor. If in-class discussion is rare or non-existent, we strongly recommend that you create your own discussion groups outside of class. The value of discussion derives partly from the fact that active learning techniques have been shown to greatly enhance students' motivation and performance in a course. Furthermore, discussion is particularly useful in philosophy since many issues are quite contentious, and being able to see the various sides of an issue is vitally important. Discussion with others, especially those with contrasting viewpoints, is one of the most efficient means for discovering opposing ideas. And finally, philosophical dialogue can be transformative because it allows for genuine exchange of ideas.

This chapter provides some helpful suggestions on making the most of discussion. More specifically, we offer the following tips.

1. Prepare for the discussion by reading and reflecting upon the assigned material. While much of philosophy is about exploring and defending your own beliefs, it is crucial to be aware of the ideas and arguments of others.

2. Challenge yourself and others by trying to adopt a view-point different from your own. A useful tool for doing this is the 'believing and doubting game'.[1] In this game, you alternately take sides of an issue, trying to find the best arguments for believing and for doubting a particular position. This works well with group discussion, but also allows you to have a discussion with yourself, so to speak.

3. Challenge yourself and others by arguing for your own beliefs rather than simply presenting an explanation of their origin. The best philosophical discussions expose your most fundamental beliefs to questioning. It is important that you try to justify these beliefs with evidence and reason. For example, if you realize that you believe God is male rather than female, try to justify this belief with a rational argument rather than simply resorting to an explanation such as, 'I grew up with this belief'.

4. Stay focused on the specific topic. Needless to say, philosophy's abstract subject matter often encourages people to go off on tangents. While this may be useful for philosophical exploration, you should try to focus discussion on a particular issue and examine it in depth.

5. Remain civil and polite. In many philosophy courses, you may be asked to discuss controversial matters that, for some students, are emotionally powerful. Ensure a respectful attitude towards others while maintaining a critical approach.

6. Encourage participation from everyone. Make sure that you listen to other people and avoid dominating the discussion. For those people who appear shy, politely ask them to express their own views.

Exercises

Instructions

For each of the following statements, play the 'believing and doubting game' with others. To begin the game, everyone in the group or class should free-write for ten minutes. Each person should use half of the time to write about why one should believe the statement and the other half to write about why one should doubt the statement. After free-writing, all members of the group should discuss their opinions keeping the six tips from the chapter in mind. A way to keep the discussion orderly and prevent it from devolving into a shouting match is to present all reasoned argument to believe the statement first and then discuss all the reasons to doubt the statement or vice versa.

1. Racial profiling is a useful, efficient and justified means of combating terrorism.
2. American universities with big-time college sports programs are exploiting their own students.
3. Human life ultimately serves no purpose.
4. There is nothing unnatural about homosexuality.
5. Incest between two consenting adults is not immoral.

5 Identifying the branches of philosophy

Philosophers, as previously mentioned, raise fundamental and open-ended questions about life and existence, questions that we categorize into a variety of types. As you begin your philosophical journey, it is helpful for you to have a basic understanding of the different types of philosophical questions. Generally speaking, philosophy has six major branches, each of which raises distinctive questions.

1. *Metaphysics* poses questions about the nature of reality and human existence, such as: What is the nature of reality? What is the relationship between mind and body? Are human decisions determined by prior events and causes or are they freely made?

   Reality

2. *Epistemology* is concerned with the possibility, sources and conditions of knowledge. It raises such questions as: How do you know what you know? What is the difference between opinion and knowledge?

   Knowledge

3. *Ethics* is the branch of philosophy posing questions about the nature of morality and how we ought to behave. It asks such questions as: Are moral standards absolute or relative? What makes an action morally praiseworthy? Is a given human practice, such as the death penalty or abortion, moral or immoral?

   Morality

4. *Political Philosophy* is concerned with the nature, extent and justification of government, as well as the role of the individual in society. Political philosophers pose such questions as: What is the source of political authority? What are the rights and duties of both governments and citizens?

   Government

5. *Philosophy of Religion* seeks answers to fundamental questions about religion, God and the afterlife. It poses such questions as: Does God exist? What is the relationship between faith and reason? Why would an all-loving God allow evil to exist? ⟧ *Religion*

6. *Logic* is the branch of philosophy concerned with evaluating philosophical arguments. Logicians ask such questions as: What is a good argument? How do I recognize a bad argument? What are the elements of good philosophical thinking? ⟧ *Mr-space*

Please note that the above list does not represent the full range and extent of philosophy, since philosophical inquiry may raise fundamental questions concerning many other aspects of life. For example, we can raise philosophical questions about the roles of sex and gender in our lives (feminist philosophy), or about the nature of art and beauty (aesthetics), or about the true claims of natural science (philosophy of science), or about the nature of sport (philosophy of sport) and so on.

Exercise

Instructions

For each of the numbered statements or questions, determine whether it falls into one or more of the following branches of philosophy: metaphysics, epistemology, ethics, political philosophy, philosophy of religion, logic. Support your determination with reasons.

⋆1. Is civil disobedience ever justified?
 2. Why is there something rather than nothing?
 3. Are selfless actions possible?
⋆4. The mind is identical to the physical processes that occur within the brain.
 5. The main purpose of government is to protect citizens from each other.
 6. God knows the future.
 7. All of my actions are predestined to happen.
 8. A valid argument is one in which the conclusion necessarily follows from the premises.

9. Does life begin at conception?
*10. How can I be certain that my senses provide accurate knowledge of the world?
11. What are the conditions under which we can call something true?
*12. Is the death penalty moral?
13. A sound argument is a valid argument with true premises.
14. A strong argument is one in which the premises likely support the conclusion.
15. Since I am determined to act as I do, I should not be held accountable for my actions.

6 Understanding metaphysics terms

Every discipline has its own language, its own unique vocabulary. If you overheard a conversation among cellular biologists, you might hear them talking about enzymes, meiosis, phagocytes, ribosomes or vacuoles. If you attended an annual convention of physicists, the following terms would likely be heard: absolute magnitude, background radiation, convection, ground states, luminosity or radiant energy. Walking through the halls of a university sociology department, you might expect to hear a variety of technical terms and phrases, such as deindustrialization, feudal societies, law of stratification, status inconsistencies and work ecology. Philosophers, likewise, have their own vocabulary and, in part, to enter into the activity of philosophy one should become familiar with philosophical terms and the ideas such terms represent.

As a student of philosophy, there are three good reasons for you to take the time not only to learn key philosophical terms, but also to learn how to use them appropriately. First, having a working knowledge of a specialized vocabulary in a discipline allows you to participate more fully and productively in that discipline. To participate in the activity of philosophy, in other words, you must learn how to 'speak like a philosopher'. Of course, you may not plan to become a professional philosopher, so you may think that learning a specialized vocabulary is not needed. Nevertheless, your philosophical learning will improve the more you become familiar with the terms and the ideas those terms represent. Second, a specialized vocabulary is useful not only for participation in a discipline, but also for efficiency in writing and speaking about philosophical ideas. For example, it is much more efficient to say, 'Thomas Hobbes is a compatibilist', than to say, 'Thomas Hobbes believes that even though human decisions are causally determined by prior causes, humans are still responsible for their decisions'. Third, from the practical point of view of being a student, when you use philosophical terms appropriately you demonstrate to your instructor a certain mastery of philosophical ideas. While we hope your motivation to learn philosophy is not strictly driven by your desire for better grades, having a working knowledge of philosophical terms can only help you in achieving academic success in philosophy.

In this chapter, we introduce you to some of the most important metaphysical terms. As mentioned in Chapter 5, *metaphysics* is the branch of philosophy that poses questions about the nature of reality and human existence, such as: What is the nature of reality? What is the relationship between mind and body? Are human decisions determined by prior events and causes or are they freely made? Below is a list of terms that you are likely to encounter if your philosophy instructor decides to spend time on metaphysical questions.

Term	Definition
Compatibilism (or soft determinism)	The dual assertion that (1) our actions are necessarily and causally determined and (2) that we are nevertheless to be held morally responsible for at least some of our actions.
Determinism	The assertion that every event is the necessary consequence of prior causes.
Eliminativism	A form of physicalism that denies the existence of a non-physical mind and also jettisons language that refers to the mind.
Functionalism	The view that mental states are constituted by the functional role they play.
Hard determinism	The dual assertion that (1) a free will is necessary for people to be held morally responsible for their actions and that (2) people do not have free will.
Idealism	A form of metaphysical monism that holds that reality is entirely mental or spiritual in nature.

Identity theory (or reductionism)	A form of physicalism asserting that claims about the mind can be reduced to claims about brain states.
Incompatibilism	The assertion that determinism is not compatible with the kind of freedom necessary for the moral evaluation of our actions.
Interactionism	A form of mind–body dualism asserting that the mind and body interact with each other even though they are distinct entities.
Libertarianism	The view that human choices are not causally determined by prior events, but are free. (Do not confuse this with the political philosophy by the same name.)
Materialism	A form of metaphysical monism asserting that reality consists of only material entities.
Metaphysical dualism	The position that reality consists of two kinds of substances.
Metaphysical monism	The position that reality consists of one kind of substance.
Mind–body dualism	The assertion that the mind and body are two separate entities.
Physicalism	The view that everything, including the human self, is physical.

Exercise

Instructions

Read the philosophical passages and then answer the questions. Provide a brief explanation for your answers. Feel free to refer back to the list of terms in the chapter as needed.

Passage 1

When it is said, that man is not a free agent, it is not pretended to compare him to a body moved by a simple impulsive cause: he contains within himself causes inherent to his existence; he is moved by an interior organ, which has its own peculiar laws, and is itself necessarily determined in consequence of ideas formed from perceptions resulting from sensations which it receives from exterior objects.[1]

Passage 2

But that determinism is incompatible with moral responsibility is as much a delusion as that it is incompatible with free will. You do not excuse a man for doing a wrong act because, knowing his character, you felt certain beforehand that he would do it. Nor do you deprive a man of a reward or prize because, knowing his goodness or his capabilities, you felt certain beforehand that he would win it.[2]

★1. Passage 1 is best described as expressing which of the following philosophical positions?

 (a) Hard determinism
 (b) Determinism
 (c) Incompatibilism
 (d) Compatibilism

2. Passage 2 is *most consonant* with which of the following philosophical positions?

 (a) Hard determinism
 (b) Incompatibilism
 (c) Determinism
 (d) Compatibilism

3. Which of the following positions is *consistent* with *both* Passages 1 and 2? Choose all that apply.

 (a) Compatibilism
 (b) Determinism
 (c) Hard determinism
 (d) Incompatibilism

4. Which of the following positions is most likely to be denied by both of the authors of Passages 1 and 2?

   (a) Compatibilism
   (b) Determinism
   (c) Hard determinism
   (d) Libertarianism

Passage 3

For this reason, from the fact that I know that I exist, and that at the same time I judge that obviously nothing else belongs to my nature or essence except that I am a thinking thing, I rightly conclude that my essence consists entirely in my being a thinking thing. And although perhaps (or rather, as I shall soon say, assuredly) I have a body that is very closely joined to me, nevertheless, because on the one hand I have a clear and distinct idea of myself, insofar as I am merely a thinking thing and not an extended thing, and because on the other hand I have a distinct idea of a body, insofar as it is merely an extended thing and not a thinking thing, it is certain that I am really distinct from my body . . . [3]

---

*5. Passage 3 is best described as expressing which of the following philosophical positions?

   (a) Mind–body dualism
   (b) Physicalism
   (c) Identity theory
   (d) Functionalism

Passage 4

When two terms belong to the same category, it is proper to construct conjunctive propositions embodying them. Thus a purchaser may say that he bought a left-hand glove and a right-hand glove, but not that he bought a left-hand glove, a right-hand glove, and a pair of gloves . . . Now the dogma of the Ghost of the Machine does just this. It maintains that there exist both bodies and minds; that there occur physical processes and mental processes; that there are mechanical causes of corporeal movements and mental causes of corporeal movements. I shall argue that these and other analogous conjunctions are absurd; but, it must be noticed, the argument will not show that either of the illegitimately conjoined propositions is absurd in itself. I am not, for example, denying that there occur mental processes. Doing long division is a mental process and so is making a joke. But I am saying that 'there occur mental processes' does not mean the same sort of thing as 'there occur physical processes', and therefore it makes no sense to conjoin or disjoin the two.[4]

6. On the basis of information provided in Passage 4, the 'dogma of the Ghost in the Machine' most likely refers to which of the following positions?

   (a) Interactionism
   (b) Identity theory
   (c) Physicalism
   (d) Functionalism

7. On the basis of information provided in Passage 4, which of the following positions is the author most likely to agree with?

   (a) Reductionism
   (b) Interactionism
   (c) Physicalism
   (d) Eliminativism

Passage 5

The intuition underlying _____ is that what determines the psychological type to which a mental particular belongs is the causal role or the particular in the mental life of the organism . . . A headache, for example, is identified with the type of mental state that among other things causes a disposition for taking aspirin in people who believe aspirin relieves a headache, causes a desire to rid oneself of the pain one is feeling, often causes someone who speaks English to say such things as 'I have a headache' . . . _____ construes the concept of the causal

> role in such a way that a mental state can be defined by its causal relations to other mental states.[5]

8. Which of the following terms would best fill in both blanks in Passage 5?

   (a) Mind–body dualism
   (b) Interactionism
   (c) Idealism
   (d) Functionalism

Passage 6

I do not pretend to be a setter-up of new notions. My endeavors tend only to unite, and place in a clearer light, that truth which was before long shared between the vulgar and the philosophers: the former being of the opinion, that those things they immediately perceive are the real things; and the latter, that the things immediately perceived, are ideas which exist only in the mind. Which two notions put together, do in effect constitute the substance of what I advance.[6]

★9. The position advocated in Passage 6 is best described as which of the following?

   (a) Materialism
   (b) Idealism
   (c) Compatibilism
   (d) Functionalism

Passage 7

The Word Body, in the most generall acceptation, signifieth that which filleth, or occupyeth some certain room, or imagined place; and dependeth not on the imagination, but is a reall part of that we call the Universe. For the Universe, being the aggregate of all Bodies, there is no reall part thereof that is not also Body.[7]

10. The position advocated in Passage 7 is best described as which of the following?

   (a) Materialism
   (b) Idealism
   (c) Mind–body dualism
   (d) Interactionism

7 Understanding epistemology terms

As mentioned in Chapter 6, there are good reasons for you to take the time not only to learn key philosophical terms, but also to learn how to use them appropriately. In this chapter, we introduce you to some of the most important terms in the branch of philosophy known as epistemology. *Epistemology* is concerned with the possibility, sources and conditions of knowledge. It raises such questions as: How do you know what you know? What is the difference between opinion and knowledge?

Below is a list of epistemological terms that you may likely encounter in a philosophy course that addresses key questions of human knowledge.

Term	Definition
A posteriori knowledge	Knowledge grounded in, or derived from, experience.
A priori knowledge	Knowledge that is gained independently of, or prior to, experience.
Coherence theory of truth	The theory that statements are true or false insofar as they cohere with a body of accepted propositions.
Constructivism	The theory that knowledge is constructed by the mind out of data given by sense experience.
Correspondence theory of truth	The theory that statements are true or false insofar as they represent the objective aspects of reality.
Empiricism	The view that the primary source of our knowledge of reality is our sense experience.

Innate ideas	Inborn ideas that we have prior to any experience.
Objectivism	The view that there are facts about the world independent of us.
Perspectivism	The theory that all facts or truths must be interpreted from one perspective or another.
Pragmatic theory of truth	The theory that the truth of propositions should be accepted to the extent that they are useful.
Primary qualities	The properties of an object that are possessed independent of any observer.
Rationalism	The view that the primary source of our knowledge of reality is the faculty of reason.
Scepticism	The view that we cannot have genuine knowledge.
Secondary qualities	The properties of an object that cause certain subjective sensations in the observer, sensations that do not accurately reflect the object.
Subjectivism	The assertion that truth is relative to each person's individual perspective.

Exercise

Instructions
Read the philosophical passages and then answer the questions. Provide a brief explanation for your answers. Feel free to refer back to the list of terms in the chapter as needed.

Passage 1

There can be no doubt that all our knowledge begins with experience . . . But though all our knowledge begins with experience, it does not follow that it all arises out of experience.[1]

---

*1. The author of Passage 1 would most likely deny which of the following positions?

(a) Scepticism
(b) Rationalism

(c) Empiricism

(d) Constructivism

2. The claims made in Passage 1 are *consistent* with which of the following positions? Choose all that apply.

(a) Scepticism

(b) Constructivism

(c) Empiricism

(d) Objectivism

Passage 2

Let us suppose the mind to be, as we say, white paper, void of all characters, without any ideas; how comes it to be furnished? Whence comes it by that cast store, which the busy and bound-less fancy of man has painted on it with an almost endless variety? Whence has it all the materials of reasons and knowledge? To this I answer, in one word, from experience. In that all our knowledge is founded, and from that it ultimately derives itself.[2]

---

3. Passage 2 is *most consonant* with which of the following philo-sophical positions?

(a) Scepticism

(b) Rationalism

(c) Empiricism

(d) Perspectivism

Passage 3

SOCRATES: Do we say that there is such a thing as the Just itself or not?

SIMMIAS: We do say so, by Zeus.

SOCRATES: And the Beautiful and the Good?

SIMMIAS: Of course.

SOCRATES: And have you even seen any of these things with your eyes?

SIMMIAS: In no way.[3]

4. Based upon his answers given to Socrates' questions in Passage 3, Simmias is most likely which of the following?

   (a) An opponent of rationalism and an advocate of scepticism
   (b) An advocate of empiricism and an opponent of scepticism
   (c) An advocate of constructivism and an opponent of rationalism
   (d) An opponent of empiricism and an advocate of rationalism

---

Passage 4

There is no logical impossibility in the hypothesis that the world sprang into being five minutes ago, exactly as it then was, with a population that 'remembered' a wholly unreal past.[4]

---

*5. To which of the following positions would the hypothesis described in Passage 4, if true, provide the most amount of support?

   (a) Scepticism
   (b) Rationalism
   (c) Empiricism
   (d) Constructivism

Passage 5

All the objects of human reason or enquiry may naturally be divided into two kinds, to wit, *Relations of Ideas* and *Matters of Fact*. Of the first kind are the science of Geometry, Algebra and Arithmetic; and, in short, every affirmation which is either intuitively or demonstratively certain . . . Propositions of this kind are discoverable by the mere operation of thought.[5]

---

6. 'Relations of Ideas', as described in Passage 5, are best interpreted as examples of which of the following?

   (a) *A priori* knowledge
   (b) *A posteriori* knowledge

(c) Primary qualities
(d) Secondary qualities

Passage 6

All that remains for me is to ask how I received this idea of God. For I did not draw it from the senses; it never came upon me unexpectedly, as is usually the case with the ideas of sensible things when these things present themselves (or seem to present themselves) to the external sense organs. Nor was it made by me, for I plainly can neither subtract anything from it nor add anything to it.[6]

---

7. The idea of God, as described in Passage 6, is best described in which of the following terms?

(a) An example of a primary quality
(b) An idea of a secondary quality
(c) An innate idea
(d) An example of *a posteriori* knowledge

Passage 7

[T]he ideas of _____ qualities of bodies are resemblances of them, and their patterns do really exist in the Bodies themselves; but the *Ideas, produced* in us *by* these _____ qualities *have no resemblance* of them at all.[7]

---

8. Which of the following pairs of terms works best to fill in the blanks, respectively, in Passage 7?

(a) Primary; primary
(b) Secondary; secondary
(c) Primary; secondary
(d) Secondary; primary

Passage 8

Minds do not *create* truth or falsehood. They create beliefs, but when once the beliefs are created, the mind cannot make them true or false, except in the special case where they concern future things which are within the power of the person believing, such as catching trains. What makes a belief true is a fact, and this fact does not (except in exceptional cases) in any way involve the mind of the person who has the belief.[8]

9. The author of Passage 8 is most likely to be which of the following?

(a) An advocate of perspectivism
(b) An advocate of objectivism and the correspondence theory of truth
(c) An opponent of objectivism
(d) An opponent of subjectivism and an advocate of the pragmatic theory of truth

Passage 9

'Facts' are justified because and as far as, while taking them as real, I am better able to deal with the incoming new 'facts' and in general to make my world wider and more harmonious. The higher and wider my structure, and the more that any particular fact or set of facts is implied in that structure, the more certain are the structure and the facts. And, if we could reach an all-embracing ordered whole, then our certainty would be absolute. But, since we cannot do this, we have to remain content with relative probability.[9]

*10. Passage 9 is *most consonant* with which of the following positions?

(a) Correspondence theory of truth
(b) Coherence theory of truth

(c) Objectivism
(d) Subjectivism

Passage 10

'Grant an idea or belief to be true,' it says, 'what concrete difference will its being true make in any one's actual life? How will the
truth be realized? What experiences will be different from those
which would obtain if the belief were false? What, in short, is the
truth's cash-value in experiential terms?'[10]

---

11. The author of Passage 10 is most likely referring to which of
the following positions?

    (a) Subjectivism
    (b) Coherence theory of truth
    (c) Objectivism
    (d) Pragmatic theory of truth

8 Understanding ethics terms

In Chapter 6, we explained why it is important for you to be able to understand and apply philosophical terms. In this chapter, we introduce you to some of the most important terms in the branch of philosophy known as ethics. *Ethics* poses questions about the nature of morality and how we ought to behave. It asks such questions as: Are moral standards absolute or relative? What makes an action morally praiseworthy? Is a given human practice, such as the death penalty or abortion, moral or immoral? The following list of ethical terms provides a good introduction to some of the main ideas of this branch of philosophy.

Term	Definition
Altruism	The view that selfless acts are possible.
Consequentialism	Any ethical theory that evaluates the morality of an act on the basis of the act's consequences.
Conventional ethical relativism	A form of ethical relativism that asserts that ethical standards are determined by the collective beliefs of a particular society.
Deontological ethics	Any ethical theory that evaluates the morality of an act on the basis of the morality of the act itself.
Ethical egoism	The theory that individuals ought to act in such a way that promotes their own interests.
Ethical hedonism	A form of ethical egoism that says humans should act to promote their own pleasure.
Ethical objectivism	The view that universal and objective ethical standards exist.

Ethical relativism	The view that no universal and objective ethical standards exist, but that all moral judgments are a matter of opinion.
Intrinsic value	The ethical or philosophical value that something has 'in itself'.
Instrumental value	The ethical or philosophical value that something has because of the ends that may be achieved by means of it.
Psychological egoism	The view that all human actions are motivated by a desire to advance one's self-interests.
Psychological hedonism	A form of psychological egoism that claims all human actions are motivated by a desire to attain pleasure and avoid pain.
Subjective ethical relativism	A form of ethical relativism that asserts that ethical standards are determined by each individual's personal beliefs.
Virtue ethics	Any ethical theory that emphasizes the character of human beings, rather than rules or consequences.

Exercise

Instructions

Read the philosophical passages and then answer the questions. Provide a brief explanation for each answer. Feel free to refer back to the list of terms in the chapter as needed.

Passage 1

Concern for the welfare of those one loves is a rational part of one's selfish interests. If a man who is passionately in love with his wife spends a fortune to cure her of a dangerous illness, it would be absurd to claim that he does it as a 'sacrifice' for her sake, not his own, and that it makes no difference to him, personally and selfishly, whether she lives or dies.[1]

---

*1. Which of the following philosophical positions will the author of Passage 1 most likely accept (on the basis of the ideas expressed in the passage)?

    (a) Altruism
    (b) Psychological egoism
    (c) Ethical hedonism
    (d) Conventional ethical relativism

2. Which one of the following philosophical positions will the author of Passage 1 least likely accept (on the basis of the ideas expressed in the passage)? Explain your answer.

    (a) Subjective ethical relativism
    (b) Psychological egoism
    (c) Ethical egoism
    (d) Altruism

Passage 2

It is a point that has been made more often in relation to ethics than in relation to psychiatry. We do not any longer make the mistake of deriving the morality of our own locality and decade directly from the inevitable constitution of human nature. We do not elevate it to the dignity of a first principle. We recognize that morality differs in every society, and is a convenient term for socially approved habits. Mankind has always preferred to say, 'It is a moral good', rather than 'It is habitual', and the fact of this preference is matter enough for a critical science of ethics.[2]

---

3. Which one of the following philosophical positions will the author of Passage 2 most likely accept?

    (a) Altruism
    (b) Subjective ethical relativism
    (c) Ethical egoism
    (d) Conventional ethical relativism

4. Which of the following philosophical positions will the author of Passage 2 least likely accept (on the basis of the ideas expressed in the passage)? Explain your answer.

   (a) Psychological egoism
   (b) Ethical objectivism
   (c) Ethical hedonism
   (d) Subjective ethical relativism

Passage 3

[T]he moral worth of an action does not lie in the effect expected from it, nor in any principle of action which requires to borrow its motive from this expected effect. For all these effects – agreeableness of one's condition and even the promotion of the happiness of others – could be brought about by other causes, so that for this there would have been no need of the will of a rational being; whereas it is in this alone that the supreme and unconditional good can be found.[3]

---

*5. The position expressed in Passage 3 is best defined as a form of which one of the following?

   (a) Consequentialism
   (b) Deontological ethics
   (c) Virtue ethics
   (d) Ethical hedonism

Passage 4

For what we do in our dealings with other people makes some of us just, some unjust; what we do in terrifying situations, and the habits of fear or confidence that we acquire, make some of us brave and others cowardly. The same is true of situations involving appetites and anger; for one or another sort of conduct in these situations makes some temperate and mild, others intemperate and irascible. To sum it up in a single account: a state [of character] results from [the repetition of] similar activities.[4]

6. The position expressed in Passage 4 is best defined as a form of which of the following?

   (a) Consequentialism
   (b) Deontological ethics
   (c) Virtue ethics
   (d) Psychological hedonism

Passage 5

The creed which accepts as the foundation of morals 'utility' or the 'greatest happiness principle' holds that actions are right in proportion as they tend to promote happiness; wrong as they tend to produce the reverse of happiness. By happiness is intended pleasure and the absence of pain; by unhappiness, pain and the privation of pleasure.[5]

---

7. The position expressed in Passage 5 is best defined as a form of which of the following?

   (a) Consequentialism
   (b) Deontological ethics
   (c) Virtue ethics
   (d) Psychological hedonism

Passage 6

The utilitarian doctrine is that happiness is desirable and [is] the only thing desirable as an end; all other things being only desirable as a means to that end.[6]

---

*8. On the basis of the information provided in Passage 6, it is reasonable to assume that happiness is which of the following?

   (a) Both an instrumental good and an intrinsic good
   (b) An intrinsic good and possibly an instrumental good
   (c) An instrumental good and possibly an intrinsic good
   (d) An instrumental good only

Passage 7

Nature has placed mankind under the governance of two sovereign masters, pain and pleasure. It is alone for them to point out what we ought to do, as well as to determine what we shall do. On the one hand the standard of right and wrong, on the other the chain of causes and effects, are fastened to their throne.[7]

9. The author of Passage 7 would most likely accept which of the following?

   (a) Consequentialism
   (b) Deontological ethics
   (c) Ethical hedonism
   (d) Virtue ethics

9 Understanding political philosophy terms

We explained in Chapter 6 why it is important for you to be able to understand and apply philosophical terms. In this chapter, we introduce you to some of the most important terms in the branch of philosophy known as political philosophy. *Political philosophy* raises questions about the nature, extent and justification of government, as well as the role of the individual in society. Political philosophers pose such questions as: What is the source of political authority? What are the rights and duties of both governments and citizens? The following list of terms introduces you to some of the main ideas of this branch of philosophy.

Term	Definition
Absolutism	The doctrine and practice of an unlimited sovereign authority to which citizens are absolutely obliged and whose power is not regulated by another authority.
Anarchism	The view that the state ought to be abolished because it is unnecessary, undesirable and/or harmful.
Aristocracy	A form of government in which those deemed the 'best' rule.
Classical liberalism	A doctrine that emphasizes the rights and freedoms of individuals and therefore promotes a limited government.
Democracy	A form of government in which the people rule, either directly by themselves or indirectly through a system of elected representatives.

Distributive justice	A form of justice related to the distribution of goods among members of a commonwealth.
Meritocracy	A form of government in which rulers are chosen based upon demonstrated talent and ability.
Political libertarianism	A doctrine that seeks to maximize individual liberty and to minimize, or even abolish, the state.
Retributive justice	A form of justice concerned with the punishment of crimes.
Social contract theory	A theory that justifies the government's authority by reference to an explicit or implicit contract made by the members of a given society.
Socialism	A political and economic theory advocating the common ownership of the means of production and of the distribution of resources.
Theocracy	A form of government in which a God or a deity (or an official representative of the divine) is recognized as the legitimate ruler.
Tyrant	A leader who abuses political power to an extreme extent.

Exercise

Instructions

Read the philosophical passages and then answer the following questions. Provide a brief explanation for each answer. Feel free to refer back to the glossary as needed.

Passage 1

The only way whereby any one divests himself of his natural liberty, and puts on the bonds of civil society, is by agreeing with other men to join and unite into a community for their comfortable, safe, and peaceable living one amongst another, in a secure enjoyment of their properties, and a greater security against any, that are not of it.[1]

*1. Which of the following philosophical positions is most consonant with Passage 1?

   (a) Theocracy
   (b) Social contract theory
   (c) Socialism
   (d) Egalitarianism

2. The author of Passage 1 is most likely to be which of the following?

   (a) An advocate of classical liberalism
   (b) An opponent of the social contract theory
   (c) An advocate of anarchism
   (d) A defender of socialism

Passage 2

Until philosophers rule as kings or those who are now called kings and leading men genuinely and adequately philosophize, that is, until political power and philosophy entirely coincide . . . cities will have no rest from evils . . . nor will the human race.[2]

---

3. The author of Passage 2 would most likely advocate for which of the following?

   (a) Anarchism
   (b) Classical liberalism
   (c) Democracy
   (d) Aristocracy

Passage 3

Private property has made us so stupid and one-sided that an object is ours only when we have it – when it exists for us as capital, or when it is directly possessed.[3]

---

4. Which of the following would the author of Passage 3 most likely accept?

(a) Classical liberalism
(b) Socialism
(c) Tyranny
(d) Aristocracy

Passage 4

Our main conclusions about the state are that a minimal state, limited to the narrow functions of protection against force, theft, fraud, enforcement of contracts, and so on, is justified; that any more extensive state will violate persons' rights not to be forced to do certain things, and is unjustified.[4]

---

*5. Which of the following would the author of Passage 4 most likely accept?

(a) Socialism
(b) Political libertarianism
(c) Anarchism
(d) Absolutism

Passage 5

The making of [a political] union consisteth in this, that every man by covenant oblige himself to some one and the same man, or to some one and the same council, by them all named and determined, to do those actions, which the said man or council shall command them to do; and to do no action which he or they shall forbid, or command them not to do.[5]

---

6. The author of Passage 5 is most likely to accept which of the following?

(a) Socialism
(b) Political libertarianism
(c) Anarchism
(d) Absolutism

7. The authors of Passages 4 and 5 would most likely agree to which of the following claims?

   (a) Classical liberalism is superior to libertarianism
   (b) Socialism is superior to libertarianism
   (c) Tyranny is desirable
   (d) Anarchism is not the best political theory

Passage 6

Unlimited power is in itself a bad and dangerous thing; human beings are not competent to exercise it with discretion.[6]

---

8. The author of Passage 6 is most likely which of the following?

   (a) An opponent of socialism
   (b) A proponent of socialism
   (c) An opponent of absolutism
   (d) A proponent of anarchism

Passage 7

So, as a prince is forced to know how to act like a beast, he must learn from the fox and the lion; because the lion is defenceless against traps and a fox is defenceless against wolves. Therefore one must be a fox in order to recognize traps, and a lion to frighten off wolves. So it follows that a prudent ruler cannot, and must not, honour his word when it places him at a disadvantage and when the reasons for which he made his promise no longer exist.[7]

---

*9. A prince who follows the advice offered in Passage 7 is likely to be which of the following?

   (a) A tyrant
   (b) An advocate of democracy
   (c) A proponent of the social contract theory
   (d) An opponent of absolutism

Passage 8

Each person is to have an equal right to the most extensive total system of equal basic liberties compatible with a similar system of liberty for all.[8]

10. Passage 8 is primarily concerned with which of the following?

(a) A principle of retributive justice
(b) A principle of distributive justice
(c) A condition of democracy
(d) A condition of meritocracy

10 Understanding philosophy of religion terms

We explained in Chapter 6 why it is important for you to be able to understand and apply philosophical terms. In this chapter, we introduce you to some of the most important terms in the branch of philosophy known as the philosophy of religion. *Philosophy of religion* seeks answers to fundamental questions about religion, God and the afterlife. It poses such questions as: Does God exist? What is the relationship between faith and reason? Why would an all-loving God allow evil to exist?

The following list of terms introduces you to some of the main ideas of this branch of philosophy.

Term	Definition
Agnosticism	The claim that we cannot know whether God exists or not due to lack of evidence.
Atheism	The claim that God does not exist.
Cosmological argument	An argument that attempts to prove that God exists from an alleged fact (or facts) about the world.
Design argument	An argument that attempts to prove that God exists from the perceived order or purpose in nature.
Evidentialism	The claim that objective evidence is required to support one's belief in God.
Fideism	The claim that faith alone justifies one's belief in God.
Monotheism	The belief that only one God exists.

Nonevidentialism	The claim that our fundamental beliefs about life do not require rational justification.
Ontological argument	An argument that attempts to prove that God exists by use of intuition and reason alone, without relying on any type of empirical evidence.
Pantheism	The belief that God is identical with nature.
Polytheism	The belief that many gods exist.
Problem of evil	The problem of trying to explain why God, who is believed to be omnipotent and all powerful, would allow evil to exist.
Theism	The claim that at least one deity exists.
Theodicy	An attempt to explain why God would allow evil to exist.

Exercise

Instructions

Read the philosophical passages and then answer the following questions. Please provide a brief explanation for each answer. Feel free to refer back to the glossary as needed.

Passage 1

Whatever knowledge is attainable, must be attained by scientific methods; and what science cannot discover, mankind cannot know.[1]

★1. Which of the following philosophical positions is most consonant with Passage 1?

(a) Monotheism
(b) Agnosticism
(c) Polytheism
(d) Nonevidentialism

Passage 2

God is the cause of all things, which are in him.[2]

Passage 3

Whatever is moved must therefore be moved by something else. If, then, that by which it is moved is itself moved, this also must be moved by something else, and this in turn by something else again. But this cannot go on forever, since there would then be no first mover, and consequently no other mover . . . We are therefore bound to arrive at a first mover which is not moved by anything, and all men understand that this is God.[3]

---

2. The author of Passage 2 is most likely which of the following?

    (a) A pantheist
    (b) An agnostic
    (c) An atheist
    (d) A polytheist

3. Passage 3 is best described as containing which of the following?

    (a) A cosmological argument
    (b) A defense of pantheism
    (c) A design argument
    (d) A description of polytheism

4. Which of the following would the author of Passage 3 most likely accept?

    (a) Atheism
    (b) Fideism
    (c) Evidentialism
    (d) Nonevidentialism

*5. The authors of both Passage 2 and Passage 3 would most likely agree on which of the following claims?

    (a) There is no good response to the problem of evil.
    (b) Theism is true and polytheism is false.

(c) Monotheism is superior to pantheism.

(d) Agosticism and nonevidentialism are both true.

Passage 4

We see how some things, like natural bodies, work for an end even though they have no knowledge. The fact that they nearly always operate in the same way, and so as to achieve the maximum good, makes this obvious, and shows us that they attain their end by design, not by chance. Now things which have no knowledge tend towards an end only through the agency of something which knows and also understands, as an arrow through an archer. There is therefore an intelligent being by whom all natural things are directed to their end.[4]

Passage 5

Why, then, should we not praise God with unspeakable praise, simply because when he made those souls who would persevere in the laws of justice, he made others who he foresaw would sin, even some who would persevere in sin? For even such souls are better than souls that cannot sin because they lack reason and free choice of the will. And these souls are in turn better than the brilliance of any material object, however splendid, which some people mistakenly worship instead of the Most High God.[5]

Passage 6

For if the God does not exist it would be of course impossible to prove it; and if he does exist it would be folly to attempt it. There is no other road to faith; if one wished to escape risk, it is as if one wanted to know with certainty that he can swim before going into the water.[6]

---

6. Passage 4 is best described as offering support for which of the following?

(a) An ontological argument

    (b) A design argument

    (c) A cosmological argument

    (d) An argument for agnosticism

7. Passage 5 is most likely written as a response to which of the following?

    (a) A cosmological argument

    (b) The problem of evil

    (c) An argument for monotheism

    (d) Fideism

8. Passage 5 is best described as which of the following?

    (a) An expression of the design argument

    (b) A criticism of theism

    (c) A defense of atheism

    (d) An example of a theodicy

★9. The author of Passage 6 is best described as which of the following?

    (a) A proponent of fideism and an opponent of nonevidentialism

    (b) A proponent of theism and an advocate of the ontological argument

    (c) A proponent of fideism and an opponent of evidentialism

    (d) An opponent of polytheism and an advocate of the design argument

10. Which of the following is not found in any of the Passages 4–6?

    (a) An ontological argument

    (b) An expression of fideism

    (c) An expression of theism

    (d) A proposed answer to the problem of evil

11 Counterfactual thinking

Philosophers are fond of using counterfactual situations (also called 'thought experiments'), which are hypothetical or imaginary scenarios often beginning with the question 'What if?' Despite the fact that such scenarios may seem completely unrealistic or bizarre, they often help improve our philosophical thinking by isolating philosophical issues by making something that is abstract concrete or by revealing our intuitions and assumptions.

Counterfactual thinking is not unique to philosophy, but other disciplines use this technique as well. For instance, a medical researcher may use counterfactual thinking to find out whether a certain medicine will help cure an infection. In such a case, the scientist is asking this counterfactual question: 'What if a person were to take this medicine – would it work?' Fortunately, for the researcher, such a question can be answered by designing an experiment to isolate variables with a control group (which does not take the medication) and an experimental group (which does). If only one person took the medicine and it seemed to work, the researcher could not be certain that the medicine was the variable responsible for curing the infection. However, with multiple subjects, we have a better chance of answering the 'what if' question because we can see the actual effects of what would happen if the medicine were taken or not.

Similarly, in philosophy, we can use counterfactual questions to isolate important variables; however, we are often left to imagine the possible consequences in an effort to answer the question because in many cases we would not want, for moral reasons, to carry out the experiment. For example, a philosopher might ask: 'What if you could find the cure to cancer by subjecting one innocent and unwilling person to experimental drugs that cause suffering and death?' Certainly, many would find such an experiment to be morally suspect.

The use of a counterfactual question might also help us understand something abstract or obscure by making it more concrete. One example of this use of counterfactual thinking is Plato's Allegory of the Cave. Plato tells a counterfactual story about prisoners in a cave. These prisoners live chained in darkness with nothing but a blank wall in front of them upon which images are cast. The prisoners' version of reality is derived from these images on the wall. According to Plato, only when they are able to get out of the cave and live in the sunlight will they truly know what is real. It is the sun, which is Plato's symbol for his idea of 'the Good', that makes this knowledge possible. By positing the sun as the source of illumination, he uses this story to give a more concrete depiction of his idea that 'the Good' is what makes the world more intelligible to those who can 'see' it. The Allegory of the Cave is not technically an argument, but it is a counterfactual scenario that serves as an illustration and elaboration of Plato's concept of 'the Good', which is abstract and difficult to understand.

Consider the following thought experiment and how it focuses our attention on the problems surrounding the idea of human choice. Imagine, for example, that on an extremely hot day you decide to eat a chocolate ice cream cone, rather than a vanilla or strawberry cone. Further imagine that after finishing the tasty treat, a visitor from the future abducts you, places you in a time machine, erases your memory of events after eating the cone, and brings you back to the exact moment when you were deciding which cone to buy. Assuming everything was exactly the same as before, is it necessary that you would choose chocolate again? As philosophy instructors, we use such thought experiments as a way of exposing our intuitions and assumptions about human freedom. If, for example, you think that you would *necessarily* make the same choice (in the *exact* same situation), this might reveal your intuition that a different choice *could not have been made* and, thus, it reveals your assumed belief that humans are not free.

The main point here is not to pursue any specific philosophical questions, but to pre-emptively defend thought experiments from the charge of being too outlandish to be useful. The unrealistic nature of many thought experiments often leads students

to discount the potential knowledge gains of reflecting on hypothetical scenarios. Yet, as we hope you come to discover, allowing
your mind to contemplate unlikely scenarios will assist you in
reflecting more deeply on perplexing philosophical questions.

Exercise

Instructions
Read each of the following passages and answer the accompanying questions.

Passage 1

[S]uppose a Man, be carried, whilst fast asleep, into a Room,
where is a Person he longs to see and speak with; and be there
locked fast in, beyond his Power to get out: he awakes and is
glad to find himself in so desirable Company, which he stays willingly in, i.e., prefers his stay to going away. I ask, Is not this stay
voluntary?[1]

---

*1. Which of the following best paraphrases the philosophical
   question raised in Passage 1? Explain your answer.

   (a) Is there a middle ground between voluntary and involun-
        tary actions?
   (b) What is the nature of voluntary actions?
   (c) Is happiness always linked to choice?

*2. Relying on your initial intuitions, respond to the following
   questions: Do you think a person who is locked in a room, but
   happy to be in the room, stays willingly? Why or why not?

*3. Passage 1 primarily concerns which of the following? Explain
   your answer.

   (a) Epistemology
   (b) Metaphysics
   (c) Ethics
   (d) Philosophy of religion

Passage 2

Suppose there were an experience machine that would give you any experience you desired. Superduper neuropsychologists could stimulate your brain so that you would think and feel you were writing a great novel, or making a friend, or reading an interesting book. All the time you would be floating in a tank, with electrodes attached to your brain. Should you plug into this machine for life, preprogramming your life's experiences?[2]

4. Which of the following best paraphrases the philosophical question raised in Passage 2?

   (a) Is an artificially constructed experience a meaningful one?
   (b) Is ignorance bliss?
   (c) Does knowledge equal power?

5. Relying on your initial intuitions, respond to the following questions: Is plugging into such an experience machine a good thing to do? Why or why not?

6. Passage 2 primarily concerns which of the following? Explain your answer.

   (a) Epistemology
   (b) Metaphysics
   (c) Ethics
   (d) Political philosophy

Passage 3

Let us examine this point and say 'God is or is not.' But which way shall we lean? Reason can settle nothing here; there is an infinite gulf between [Christians and atheists]. A game is on, at the other end of this infinite distance, and heads or tails will turn up. What will you wager? . . . Let us weigh gain and loss in calling heads that God is. Reckon these two chances: if you win, you win all; if you lose, you lose naught.[3]

7. Which of the following most accurately paraphrases the philosophical question raised in Passage 3?

   (a) Can we prove that God exists?
   (b) Is it more likely that God exists than not?
   (c) What are the positive and negative consequences of believing in God?

8. Relying on your initial intuitions, respond to the following questions: Should one believe in God simply because it might be beneficial? Why or why not?

9. Passage 3 primarily concerns which of the following? Explain your answer.

   (a) Philosophy of religion
   (b) Logic
   (c) Ethics
   (d) Political philosophy

Passage 4

[S]uppose it were like this: people-seeds drift about in the air like pollen, and if you open your windows, one may drift in and take root in your carpets or upholstery. You don't want children, so you fix up your windows with fine mesh screens, the very best you can buy. As can happen, however, on very, very rare occasions does happen, one of the screens is defective; and a seed drifts in and takes root. Does the person-plant who now develops have a right to the use of your house?[4]

---

10. Which of the following most accurately paraphrases the philosophical question raised in Passage 4?

    (a) When does life begin?
    (b) Does a fetus have a right to life?
    (c) What are the consequences of accidental pregnancy?

11. Relying on your initial intuitions, respond to the following questions: Does the 'person-plant' have a right to use your house? Why or why not?

12. Passage 4 primarily concerns which of the following? Explain your answer.

   (a) Epistemology
   (b) Metaphysics
   (c) Ethics
   (d) Logic

Passage 5

Brown, Jones, and Smith enter the hospital for brain rejuvenations. (In a brain rejuvenation, one's brain is removed, its circuitry is analyzed by a fabulous machine, and a new brain is put back in one's skull, just like the old one in all relevant respects, but built of healthier grey matter. After a brain rejuvenation one feels better, and may think and remember more clearly, but the memories and beliefs are not changed in content.) Their brains are removed and placed on the brain cart. The nurse accidentally over turns the cart; the brains of Brown and Smith are ruined. To conceal his tragic blunder, the nurse puts Jones's brain through the fabulous machine three times, and delivers the duplicates back to the operating room. Two of these are put in the skulls that formerly belonged to Brown and Smith. Jones's old heart has failed and, for a time, he is taken for dead. In a few hours, however, two individuals wake up, each claiming to be Jones, each happy to be finally rid of his headaches. But somewhat upset at the drastic changes that seem to have taken place in his body. We shall call these persons 'Smith-Jones' and 'Brown-Jones.' The question is, who are they?[5]

---

13. Which of the following most accurately paraphrases the philosophical question raised in Passage 5?

   (a) What is the relationship between mind and matter?
   (b) Are brain rejuvenations morally permissible?
   (c) What is personal identity?

14. Relying on your initial intuitions, respond to the following questions: Does the person named 'Jones' still exist? Why or why not?

15. Passage 5 primarily concerns which of the following? Explain your answer.

    (a) Epistemology
    (b) Metaphysics
    (c) Ethics
    (d) Logic

12 Understanding philosophical claims

Philosophers often make a variety of *claims*, that is, they assert that something either is, or ought to be, the case. Such claims come in different forms, and knowledge of these forms makes us not only better prepared to understand the claims, but also to evaluate them. Claims are the basic building blocks of arguments, and arguments are the primary vehicle philosophers use to justify their positions and theories (for more on arguments, see Chapters 14–19). Thus, before we can understand and evaluate arguments, we must be able to understand and evaluate the claims contained within those arguments. For the present purposes, we will only concern ourselves with two basic distinctions among claims, namely, the distinction between *descriptive* and *normative* claims and the one between *a priori* and *a posteriori* claims.

Before talking about these distinctions, however, we must determine whether a sentence counts as a claim. In order to count as a claim, the sentence must be claiming that something is true. Notice that some sentences are not claims in this sense. For example, 'stop the car!' is not making a truth claim, but is instead commanding someone to act in a certain way. 'Are you happy?' is also not a claim, but it is a question. By contrast, 'the car is blue' is claiming that it is true that the car is blue. Of course, not all claims are actually true since someone might make a false claim. In either case, we can say that a claim is capable of being true or false, and we call this characteristic 'truth aptness'. A claim, then, is truth apt because it is capable of being true or false in some contexts. A useful way to determine whether a sentence is a claim is to insert the sentence into the following formula: 'It is true/false that _____ '. If the resulting sentence is a coherent sentence, then the sentence is likely a claim. 'It is true that "stop the car!"' is not coherent, for example.

Now that we know how to determine whether a sentence is a claim, we can make the following distinction: a descriptive claim *describes* that something *is* the case, while a normative claim *prescribes* what *ought* to be the case. Examples of descriptive claims include: 'the sun will rise tomorrow', 'God is good' and 'tables often have four legs'. Examples of normative claims include: 'The death penalty ought to be abolished', 'you should give to charity' and 'one must tell the truth'. At first glance, one might think that a normative claim is not truth apt since it is claiming that something *ought* to be the case, rather than *is* the case. However, a normative claim is actually claiming that something is true. For example, a person claiming that the death penalty ought to be abolished is claiming 'it is true that the death penalty ought to be abolished'. It is also important to note, at this point, that normative claims (or 'ought statements') are not always based on morality, but may be grounded in other normative systems, such as law or fashion. For example, in some places, a fashion rule might be that 'one ought not to wear chequered pants with a striped shirt'. While this might be a normative claim, it is not one of morality. One would not be morally wrong, in other words, if one sported such a combination of clothes.

Philosophers also make a distinction between *a priori* and *a posteriori* claims. An *a priori* claim seems to be true by virtue of its terms, that is, either by definition or by the relation of its terms to each other. For example, a 'square has four sides' seems to be obviously true given the definition of a square. Other examples of *a priori* claims that seem true by definition include: 'all bachelors are unmarried males', 'justice ought to be pursued' and 'all extended bodies occupy space'. An example of an *a priori* claim, true by relation of its terms to each other, is '4+2=6'. *A posteriori* claims, on the other hand, seem true or false by virtue of experience. For example, the 'earth is round' is an *a posteriori* claim because it can be affirmed or denied on the basis of empirical evidence. Other examples of *a posteriori* claims include: 'force equals mass times acceleration', 'smoking is healthy' and 'snow is white'.

It is important to be able to distinguish between types of claims in part because it helps in understanding how to evaluate those claims. For example, to confirm that an *a priori* claim is true, one needs only to properly understand the terms involved in the claim. By contrast, to evaluate an *a posteriori* claim, one must turn to experience with the hope of confirming or denying the claim. In Chapter 13, we will discuss more fully the process of evaluating claims. For now, we will focus on the more fundamental skill of understanding types of claims.

So far we have mentioned truth in passing, but we should pause to discuss the philosophical aspects of truth. Certainly, an important job for philosophers is to determine whether claims are true or false. Depending on the claim, the difficulty or ease of determining its truth value varies widely. Consider the difference between these two claims, one descriptive and one normative: 'water boils at 100° Celsius' and 'we should never kill other human beings'. The first claim is relatively uncontroversial, and we would be able to verify this through empirical observation. However, when we consider the second claim, we realize that the truth value of this claim is less certain. There are very few, if any, normative claims that everyone will agree upon, but we could obtain consensus on many empirical claims.

Clearly, one's background knowledge or theories will affect how one evaluates many claims, both descriptive and normative. For example, if you have a comprehensive understanding of physics and chemistry, you will know that the truth of the descriptive claim about the boiling point of water is only true at sea level or at an air pressure of 15 psi. Regarding the claim about killing humans, a pacifist will certainly assign a different truth value than a soldier or policeman, who believes that sometimes killing, though unfortunate, is necessary.

Exercises

Part A

Instructions
Determine whether each of the following sentences is a claim.

    ★1. It is wrong to torture human babies just for fun.
    2. Go team!
    3. You should file your taxes by 15 April.
    ★4. What is the deadline for submitting tax forms to the government?
    5. $E = mc^2$.

Part B

Instructions
Determine whether each of the following claims is descriptive or normative.

    ★1. The sky is blue.
    2. You should adopt a vegan diet.
    3. My mother said, 'You ought to tell the truth.'
    4. Telling the truth is good for everybody.
    ★5. One ought to stop at red lights.

Part C

Instructions
Determine whether each of the following claims is *a priori* or *a posteriori*.

    ★1. Most books are made of paper.
    2. If I am thinking, then I must exist.
    3. Every effect has a cause.
    4. All swans are white.
    ★5. Triangles have three interior angles.

13 Evaluating philosophical claims

Philosophers, as we have seen, make a variety of claims about fundamental matters in our lives. It is essential to the philosophical enterprise not simply to make claims, but to make *good* claims. In reading philosophy, one of your main goals is to evaluate the merit of the philosophical claims that you encounter. More to the point, the critical aspect of philosophical activity relies on the ability to find and evaluate such claims. Philosophers may disagree about the details regarding the evaluation of claims, but most are likely to agree that a philosophical claim ought to be:

1. Clear
2. Consistent
3. Compelling
4. Supported by good arguments

In this chapter we will only focus on the first three criteria. It is important to keep in mind that claims usually need *arguments* to justify belief in them (see Chapters 14–19), but before you can understand what counts as a good argument, you have to understand what counts as a clear, consistent and compelling claim.

Ideally, philosophers would provide a clear explanation of their ideas by doing such things as defining key terms, providing examples, using terms consistently and avoiding esoteric jargon. Their claims, in other words, ought to be clear and easily understood. If one claims, for example, that all humans are selfish, one ought to clearly define what is meant by the term 'selfish'. Or, as another example, instead of saying 'avoid esoteric jargon' above, we could have said 'use plain language'. Unfortunately, you might find that many philosophers fail to be as clear as they could be, but we should still strive for clarity ourselves and still expect it from others.

Philosophers are also expected to make claims that are consistent and/or not contradictory with other claims they have made. Two claims are *inconsistent* with each other when both of them cannot be true at the same time. If I claim, at the same time (and in the same place), that 'I weigh 165 pounds' and 'I weigh 175 pounds', I am asserting inconsistent claims because both of these claims cannot be true simultaneously. Two claims are *contradictory* when they have opposite truth-values. To put it another way, two claims are contradictory when the truth of one implies the falsity of the other and vice versa. 'No animals are rational', for example, contradicts 'some animals are rational' because one of them will be true whenever the other is false and vice versa.

When evaluating philosophical claims, you should also determine whether they are *compelling*. A claim is compelling if it is true or at least probable. The method for determining whether a claim is compelling depends upon the type of claim it is. The evidential support required for a claim to be true depends, largely, on the type of claim that it happens to be (see Chapter 12). A descriptive *a posteriori* claim, for example, must square with evidence from our experience to be compelling. 'Water freezes at 32 degrees Fahrenheit' is compelling because it seems true on the basis of our experience of the world. A normative *a priori* claim, on the other hand, must square with our intuitions to be compelling. If you have the intuition that all life has equal value, then 'You ought to protect all life equally' would be a compelling claim because its truth seems to follow from your intuition.

In contrast to clarity and consistency, the determination of whether a claim is compelling is not a onetime judgement, but an ongoing assessment at the heart of the philosophical practice. One's understanding or intuitions of the world may be incomplete or wrong and may need to be revised or rejected. In certain contexts, for example, the claim that water freezes at 32 degrees Fahrenheit is not true. Also, while one might have the intuition that human life is more valuable than other forms of life, someone might provide evidence against your original intuition through an argument that reveals a counter intuition that all life has equal value. For example, the fact that most adults would willingly sacrifice their lives for their children suggests that most people do not believe that all human life has equal value. In both of these cases, then, a claim that first appeared compelling might later be rejected. The opposite is also true. Many of the claims that you will find in philosophy may not, at first, strike you as compelling because they seem out of joint with your understanding of the world and your intuitions. Yet, upon further reflection, you may decide that such claims have merit. David Hume's famous claim that we have insufficient reason to believe that the sun will rise tomorrow is a good example of this point. It is for this very reason that you should be suspicious of your own or any others' (including *any* philosophers') judgements about a particular claim being compelling without examining the claim carefully.

Exercise

Part A
Instructions
Determine whether each pair of claims is inconsistent, contradictory or neither.

★1. (a) Some humans are rational.
   (b) Not all humans are rational.
2. (a) Natural rights do not exist.
   (b) Some natural rights exist.
3. (a) Bill is in favour of the death penalty.
   (b) Bill voted for a senator who opposes the death penalty.
4. (a) All animals are selfish.
   (b) No animals are selfish.
★5. (a) All Cretans are liars.
   (b) The Cretan named Epimenides is not a liar.

Part B
Instructions
For each of the passages below, read the passage and then answer the questions that follow.

1. Are the main philosophical claims of the passage *clearly* expressed? If not, what claims are not clear?
2. Are these main claims *compelling*? That is, do the claims seem true or probable? If not, which claims are not compelling?

3. Does the author make any claims that are *inconsistent* or *contradictory* with other claims in the passage? If so, which claims are they?

---

*Passage 1

To fear death, gentlemen, is no other than to think oneself wise when one is not, to think one knows what one does not know. No one knows whether death may be the greatest of all blessings for a man, yet men fear it as if they knew that it is the greatest of evils. And surely it is the most blameworthy ignorance to believe that one knows what one does not know . . . Let us reflect in this way, too, that there is good hope that death is a blessing, for it is one of two things: either the dead are nothing and have no perception of anything, or it is, as we are told, a change and a relocating for the soul from here to another place. If it is a complete lack of perception, like a dreamless sleep, then death would be a great advantage. For I think that if one had to pick out that night during which a man slept soundly and did not dream, put beside it other nights and days of his life, and then see how many days and nights had been better and more pleasant than that night, not only a private person but a great king would find them easy to count compared with the other days and nights. If death is like this I say it is an advantage, for all eternity would then seem to be no more than a single night. If, on the other hand, death is a change from here to another place, and what we are told is true and all who have died are there, what greater blessing could there be . . . ?[1]

Passage 2

Many have dreamed up republics and principalities which have never in truth been known to exist; the gulf between how one should live and how one does live is so wide that a man who neglects what is actually done for what should be done learns the way to self-destruction rather than self-preservation. The fact is that a man who wants to act virtuously in every way necessarily comes to grief among so many who are not virtuous.[2]

Passage 3

Will to truth is a making firm, a making true and durable, an abolition of the false character of things, a reinterpretation of it into beings. 'Truth' is therefore not something there, that might be found or discovered – but something that must be created and that gives a name to a process, or rather to a will to overcome that has in itself no end . . . not a becoming-conscious of something that is in itself firm and determined.[3]

Passage 4

If I am a workingman and choose to join a Christian trade-union rather than be a communist, and if by being a member I want to show that the best thing for man is resignation, that the kingdom of man is not of this world, I am not only involving my own case – I want to be resigned for everyone. As a result, my action has involved all humanity. To take a more individual matter, if I want to marry, to have children, even if this marriage depends solely on my own circumstances or passion or wish, I am involving all humanity in monogamy and not merely myself. Therefore, I am responsible for myself and everyone else. I am creating a certain image of man of my own choosing. In choosing myself, I choose man.[4]

Passage 5

We are still far from pondering the essence of action decisively enough. We view action only as causing an effect. The actuality of the effect is valued according to its utility. But the essence of action is accomplishment. To accomplish means to unfold something into the fullness of its essence, to lead it forth into this fullness – producere. Therefore only what already is can really be accomplished. But what 'is' above all is Being. Thinking accomplishes the relation of Being to the essence of man. It does not make or cause the relation. Thinking brings this relation to Being solely as something handed over to it from Being. Such offering consists in the fact that in thinking Being comes to language.[5]

14 Understanding arguments

One of the main tasks of philosophers is to present arguments that support their ideas or theories. An argument in philosophy is a series of claims in which one of the claims (i.e., the conclusion) is said to follow from, or be supported by, one or more of the other claims (i.e., the premises). An important defining feature of arguments is their *inferential* nature. In other words, on the basis of the supposed truth of the premises, philosophers *infer* the truth of the conclusion. For example, a philosopher might argue that it is wrong for states to execute criminals, even if the criminals are guilty of heinous crimes, because (1) such punishment is considered cruel and unusual and (2) cruel and unusual punishment is wrong. In this case, the philosopher *infers* the *conclusion* (i.e., capital punishment is wrong) from the *premises* (i.e., capital punishment is cruel and unusual; cruel and unusual punishment is wrong).

To properly understand an argument and to identify its inference, one must be able to distinguish between the premises and the conclusion of an argument. Fortunately, this task is made easier by the fact that philosophers often (though not always) use *premise* and/or *conclusion indicators* when they argue. A premise indicator is a term that usually precedes a premise, such as *since, because, for, seeing that* or *given that*. Similarly, a conclusion indicator is a term that indicates a conclusion is about to follow. Conclusion indicators include, among others, terms such as *therefore, hence, it follows that* and *thus*. Here are a couple of short arguments that include indicator words:

- *Because* (premise) animals can suffer and (premise) the capacity to suffer is a condition for ethical treatment, *therefore* (conclusion) they deserve ethical treatment.
- *Since* (premise) you can eat your brain but you cannot eat your mind, *thus* (conclusion) the mind and brain are different.

In the above examples, the conclusion comes after the premises. It should be noted, however, that the conclusion of an argument might be stated first, as in the following example.

- (conclusion) Capital punishment is a suitable punishment for mass murders *given that* (premise) mass murderers forfeit their natural rights by killing innocent people.

Note also that indicator words need not be present for an argument to be made, but an argument always requires an *inferential* connection between premises and conclusion. That is, a philosophical arguer always *infers* that something is the case on the basis of something else being the case.

One difficulty to mention here is that philosophers might leave unstated one of the claims in an inferential link, thereby forcing the reader to supply it. As we use the term, an *enthymeme* is an argument in which one of the claims is not explicitly stated. For example, consider the following argument.

Premise: The death penalty causes the death of innocent people.
Conclusion: Therefore, the death penalty is clearly wrong.

The above argument leaves unstated an important claim, namely, 'Something is wrong if it causes the death of innocent people'. This unstated premise supplies a logical link from the stated premise to the conclusion.

Stated Premise: The death penalty results in the death of innocent people.
Unstated Premise: Something is wrong if it results in the death of innocent people.
Conclusion: Therefore, the death penalty is wrong.

There are many reasons why an author might leave a premise unstated. For example, in some cases, the premise might seem so uncontroversial that it is not worth stating. In other cases, however, philosophers might leave out a premise in an effort to avoid stating a controversial premise and thereby protect themselves from criticism. Premises might also be assumed because the philosopher is not presenting his or her argument carefully enough. Additionally, an author might intentionally leave out a premise for rhetorical effect. In any case, to properly understand (and evaluate) an argument, it is necessary to bring into view both the stated and unstated claims.

Once you've identified the premises and conclusion of an argument, it is helpful to put the argument into *standard form*. An argument in standard form is one in which the premises and conclusions are numbered in logical order and the conclusion is separated from the premises by a line. For example, here is an argument in standard form.

1. My idea of God did not arise from sense experience.
2. If my idea of God did not arise from sense experience, then it must be innate.
_____

3. Thus, my idea of God is innate.

As we shall see in Chapter 16, it is much easier to evaluate an argument once the premises and conclusion are clearly laid out and marked.

Exercises

Part A
Instructions
Supply the missing claim for each of the following enthymemes and indicate whether the missing claim is a premise or conclusion.

   ★1. Philosophy does not provide definitive answers, thus it is a worthless discipline.
   2. The *Bible* is our greatest source of moral knowledge. Thus, legislators ought to rely on it when crafting laws.
   3. Euthanasia offers a suffering person a justifiable way to end her pain. For this reason, it ought to be legally permitted.
   4. Certainly, the *Constitution* is the guiding document for our country, and the guiding document for our country ought to be cherished.

5. Racial profiling must be stopped because it is a moral travesty.
6. Children are the future of humanity, so they ought to be provided with a strong education.
7. Animals are capable of great suffering. Any creatures capable of great suffering deserve to be treated with respect.
8. Corporations are not evil since they provide jobs for many people.
9. Because tenure encourages professors to be lazy and unconcerned for their students' education, it ought to be abolished.
10. Astrology is a pseudo-science with no evidence to support it. Thus, people should stop relying on astrologers for advice.

Part B

Instructions

Identify the premises and the conclusion of the argument in each of the following passages. Furthermore, supply missing premises or conclusions when needed and put the arguments into standard form. Note that some of the sentences are not premises or conclusions in the argument.

*Passage 1

In recent years, more women have joined military service in the United States than in previous years. However, their actions in the military are restricted to a certain extent because they are not allowed to join combat units. Is this right? It seems to me that women, for the most part, do not have the strength necessary to perform effectively in combat. It follows that women should continue to be barred from such operations.

Passage 2

Everything that happens in the universe has a cause. Does it not make sense, for example, that there was a cause of the Big Bang? And if something caused the Big Bang, does it not make sense that there is a cause of that cause? But, the series of causes cannot go backwards to infinity. Thus, there must be a first cause that started everything.

Passage 3

Our lawmakers should prohibit children from playing violent video games. It is obvious that such games make children more likely to commit violence themselves. Our society needs less violence, not more.

Passage 4

Homosexuality is a sin against God. Our Holy Book claims that men should not sleep with men and that women should not sleep with women. Because our moral system relies upon the decrees of God, and because our Holy Book is the word of God, it follows that homosexuality must not be practised.

Passage 5

The only arguments against the legalization of gay marriage are grounded in religious belief. Many religious fanatics all around the world cling to their negative views of homosexuality to practise a form of discrimination. Religious belief, however, is not a legitimate ground upon which to establish public policies. Thus, homosexuals who wish to be married ought to be allowed to do so.

15 Understanding argument types

Recall from Chapter 14 that an argument in philosophy is a series of statements in which one of the statements (i.e., the conclusion) is said to follow inferentially from, or be supported by, one or more of the other statements (i.e., the premises). Arguments can be divided into two main types: deductive and inductive. A *deductive argument* is one in which the conclusion is supposed to follow from the premises *necessarily*. The author of the argument, in other words, *claims* that the conclusion, as a matter of logic, necessarily follows from the premises.

Example of deductive argument

Premise 1: Female soldiers have the skills and talent required for combat.

Premise 2: Any soldiers with the skills and talent required for combat should be allowed to join a combat unit.

Conclusion: Thus, female soldiers should be allowed to join a combat unit.

The author of the above argument is claiming that if the premises are true, then the conclusion is *necessarily* true. Contrast the deductive argument above with the following inductive argument.

Example of inductive argument

Premise 1: Most female soldiers have the skills and talent required for combat.

Premise 2: Major Susan Smith is a female soldier.

Conclusion: Major Susan Smith probably has the skills and talent required for combat.

In an inductive argument, the arguer is claiming that the conclusion *probably* follows from the premises. The difference between a deductive and an inductive argument, then, is that in the former the premises are said to render the conclusion logically necessary, while in the latter the premises are said to render the conclusion likely or probable.

When determining whether an argument is deductive or inductive, you should look for indicator words (such as 'necessarily' or 'probably') since these provide a generally reliable guide for distinguishing between the two types of argument. However, it is possible that indicator words are absent or mistakenly used. In such a case, you need to look at the actual strength of the *inference* between premises and conclusion. For example, consider the following argument.

> *Premise 1*: Most female soldiers have the skills and talent necessary for combat.
> *Premise 2*: Major Susan Smith is a female soldier.
> *Conclusion*: Major Susan Smith must have the skills and talent necessary for combat.

In the above argument, the inference between the premises and the conclusion is probable at best, thus the argument is an inductive one. However, by using the word 'must', the author of the argument seems to be claiming that the conclusion necessarily follows from the premises. For cases such as these, the proper categorization of the argument should be based on the inferential link and not simply the author's indicator words or lack thereof.

When you begin to read and write philosophical arguments, you might encounter a series of arguments combined into what we call an *extended* argument (otherwise known as chain or complex argument). Extended arguments are not a different type of argument, but a series of arguments that are logically connected. While the arguments above have only a few premises and can be expressed in just a few sentences, extended arguments occur across broader stretches of text and may often include a combination of inductive and deductive arguments. In an extended argument, one claim could serve as both a premise and a conclusion within the same string of arguments. The following is an example of an extended argument wherein some claims can be seen to function as both premise and conclusion.

Example of an extended argument

Premise: Female soldiers have the skills and talent required for combat.

Premise: Any soldiers with the skills and talent required for combat should be allowed to join a combat unit.

Conclusion/Premise: Thus, female soldiers should be allowed to join a combat unit.

Premise: If female soldiers should be allowed to join a combat unit, then the US Army ought to change their regulations to allow women to fight in combat units.

Conclusion/Premise: The US Army ought to change their regulations to allow women to fight in combat units.

Premise: Male soldiers will likely resist the inclusion of women in combat units.

Premise: Such resistance will likely cause problems with implementing new regulations.

Conclusion/Premise: Thus, the US Army should probably try to overcome that resistance to avoid problems of implementation.

Premise: Such resistance is best overcome through a gradual training process.

Main Conclusion: Thus, the US Army should follow a gradual training process before making changes to regulations concerning women's role in combat.

Notice that the example of an extended argument above employs both deductive and inductive arguments in its path to the main conclusion.

Exercises

Part A: Deductive and inductive arguments
Instructions
Determine whether each of the following passages contains an argument and, if so, whether the argument is best categorized as deductive or inductive.

*1. If smoking cigarettes is more dangerous than smoking marijuana, then smoking marijuana should be legally permitted. Smoking cigarettes is more dangerous than smoking marijuana. Thus, smoking marijuana should be legally permitted.

2. The mind is indivisible. The body is divisible. Something cannot be both divisible and indivisible at the same time. It follows, then, that the mind and the body are not the same thing.

3. If you break the law, then you might get caught.

4. It is a fact that men are taller than women. John Jay is therefore taller than his wife.

*5. Most studies concerning the effectiveness of the death penalty conclude that the death penalty does not offer an effective deterrent to capital crimes.

6. If God is omnipotent, then he should be able to create a stone that he cannot lift. He is not able to create a stone that he cannot lift. Hence, God is not omnipotent.

7. The universe operates according to strict scientific laws. It is unlikely that these laws just happened to come about by chance. Thus, a divine intelligence is probably responsible for creating scientific laws.

8. Euthanasia is clearly wrong. After all, suicide is morally wrong and euthanasia is a form of suicide.

*9. A perfect society is a just society. It is the case, then, that a just society is a perfect society.

10. Shaquille O'Neal believes the new Spalding basketball is superior to the old ball used by the National Basketball Association. It follows that the new ball is better.

Part B: Extended arguments

Instructions

The following claims are part of an extended argument. Put them into a logical sequence of premises and conclusions, all leading to one final conclusion.

1. Killing is not always wrong.
2. If killing is always wrong, then victims of rape are wrong to have an abortion.
3. Abortion is not always wrong.
4. If killing is always wrong, then abortion is always wrong.
5. If abortion is always wrong, then victims of rape are wrong to have an abortion.
6. It is not wrong for victims of rape to have an abortion.

16 Evaluating arguments

As we have seen in Chapter 13, the evaluation of a philosophical claim involves determining whether the claim is clear, compelling, consistent and supported by good arguments. In this chapter, we explain how to determine whether claims are supported by good arguments. To critically evaluate a philosophical argument, you ought to determine whether it is both *logically correct* and *good*. A *logically correct* argument is one in which the premises entail or support the conclusion. A *good* argument is a logically correct argument that also has true premises.

To determine whether an argument is logically correct, *assume* that the premises are true and then ask whether the conclusion is *entailed* by or *supported* by the premises. If the conclusion follows from the premises, the argument is *valid* (for deductive arguments) or *strong* (for inductive arguments). A logically correct argument, then, is either *valid* or *strong*, depending upon whether the argument is deductive or inductive, respectively (see Chapter 15 for the difference between deductive and inductive arguments). If an argument is not logically correct, it is either *invalid* (for deductive arguments) or *weak* (for inductive arguments).

To say an argument is logically correct, however, does not necessarily mean it is a good argument; it is to say that the premises logically entail or support the conclusion. To determine whether an argument is good, we must determine whether the premises of a logically correct argument are true. If an argument is logically correct and it has true premises, then it is a *good* argument, that is, *sound* (for deductive arguments) or *cogent* (for inductive arguments). In this case, a reasonable person ought to accept the conclusion of a sound argument as true or the conclusion of a cogent argument as probable.

Exercise

Part A

Instructions

Determine whether the following deductive arguments are valid or invalid.

---

*Argument 1

1. Each and every human being is immortal.
2. Tony Blair is a human being.

3. Thus, Tony Blair is immortal.

Argument 2

1. Baseball is a pastime.
2. All pastimes are enjoyable.

3. Therefore, baseball is enjoyable.

Argument 3

1. All ripe fruit are edible.
2. All bananas are ripe fruit.

3. Therefore, all bananas are edible.

Argument 4

1. War kills innocent civilians.
2. It is always unjustified to kill innocent civilians.

3. Therefore, war is always unjustified.

---

*Argument 5

1. My sister has seven siblings.

2. Therefore, at least two of my siblings were born on the same day of the week.

Part B

Instructions

Determine whether the following deductive arguments are sound or unsound.

---

*Argument 6

1. Each and every human being is mortal.
2. Barack Obama is a human being.

---

3. Thus, Barack Obama is mortal.

Argument 7

1. All apples are red fruit.
2. All strawberries are red fruit.

---

3. Therefore, all apples are strawberries.

Argument 8

1. The Empire State Building is taller than the Eiffel Tower.
2. The Taj Mahal is shorter than the Empire State Building.

---

3. Therefore, the Taj Mahal is shorter than the Eiffel Tower.

Argument 9

1. London is in England.
2. England is in Europe.

---

3. Therefore, London is in Europe.

---

*Argument 10

1. If the temperature drops below −5°C, water on the ground will freeze.
2. If it snows, the temperature will drop below −5°C.

---

3. Therefore, if it snows, then water on the ground will freeze.

Part C

Instructions

Determine whether the following inductive arguments are strong or weak.

---

*Argument 11

1. Apples are usually sweeter than carrots.
2. A banana is not a carrot.

   ---

3. Thus, apples are probably not sweeter than bananas.

Argument 12

1. Every June for over 200 years, it has not rained in London.

   ---

2. Therefore, chances are it will not rain in London next June.

Argument 13

1. Most maps of the United States show Oregon bordering Texas.

   ---

2. Therefore, it is probably true that Oregon borders Texas.

Argument 14

1. Steve has a convertible car that runs well.
2. Larry recently purchased a convertible car.

   ---

3. Therefore, Larry's convertible car will probably run well.

---

*Argument 15

1. Tiger Woods is the world's best golfer.
2. Tiger Woods says the Super Max golf ball is very good.

   ---

3. Therefore, the Super Max golf ball is probably very good.

Part D

Instructions

Determine whether the following inductive arguments are cogent or not cogent.

---

*Argument 16

1. Fruits are usually sweeter than vegetables.
2. Apples are fruits.
3. Cauliflower is a vegetable.

---

4. Thus, apples are probably sweeter than cauliflower.

Argument 17

1. Many cities have professional ice hockey teams.
2. Paris is a city.

---

3. Therefore, Paris probably has a professional ice hockey team.

Argument 18

1. The moon has been orbiting the earth for billions of years.

---

2. Therefore, it is likely that ten years from now, the moon will still be orbiting the earth.

Argument 19

1. Insects are capable of rational reflection.
2. Beings capable of rational reflection can communicate with each other.

---

3. Therefore, insects are capable of communicating with each other.

---

*Argument 20

1. Boris Becker is the world's best golfer.
2. Boris Becker says the Super Max golf ball is very good.

---

3. Therefore, the Super Max golf ball is probably very good.

17 Arguments by analogy

A common way that philosophers argue for a particular conclusion is by using an argument by analogy. Although arguments by analogy are a form of inductive arguments, their common use encourages us to dedicate a separate chapter to understanding and evaluating them. In an argument by analogy, the arguer draws a comparison between two or more things and uses the relevant similarities among these things to draw a conclusion. Such arguments can be effective only if the objects held in comparison are relevantly similar. Both objects held in comparison, the analogues, must be similar in ways that are relevant to the conclusion for which the analogy argues; such arguments will have the following form:

Form of arguments by analogy

1. X is like Y
2. Y has a particular characteristic Z

---

3. Thus, X also has Z

An argument from analogy is especially effective as a means for supporting a controversial claim. By first pointing out an uncontroversial claim that most people would accept, the arguer draws an analogy between the controversial and the uncontroversial claims through the presence of some relevantly similar property or claim. Here's an example of an argument by analogy in which someone might argue for the controversial claim that cows have natural rights:

Example of an argument by analogy

1. Cows are similar to humans in that they have the capacity to suffer.
2. Humans have natural rights that protect them from unnecessary suffering.

---

3. Thus, cows also have natural rights.

In the above example, the arguer probably believes that cows are relevantly similar to humans and therefore have the same rights as humans. Here we can see how analogical arguments are especially useful in controversial cases. As the above example illustrates, someone might try to argue for vegetarianism by claiming that cows, and other animals eaten by humans, have rights similar to those of humans. The claim that it is wrong for us to practise cannibalism is an uncontroversial one. However, once we consider, as the argument suggests, what it is about human beings that makes it wrong for us to eat other humans, we focus on our common ability to suffer. Thus, some claim that humans, because they are capable of suffering, have certain natural rights. The vegetarian now, by analogy, points out that one analogue, cows, are capable of suffering. Cows, in other words, are relevantly similar to the second analogue, humans, because they can suffer. Since our capacity to suffer is the ground for our right not to be killed and eaten, according to this argument, and since cows have this same characteristic, one could argue that cows have the same right not to be killed and eaten.

The best way to critically evaluate arguments by analogy is to consider whether the analogy works by questioning whether the two (or more) analogues are relevantly similar or relevantly dissimilar. Let us consider the example argument. To begin, we might ask: 'In what ways are cows and humans similar?', 'In what ways are they dissimilar?', 'Do their similarities or dissimilarities support or count against the attribution of certain natural rights to both?' Of course, cows and humans are similar in many ways: they are mammals, they have eyes, they walk around, they have brains, they suffer, they feel pleasure and so on. They are also dissimilar in many ways: cows, for example, cannot perform algebraic equations, cannot build cars, cannot fly an airplane and so on. It is important to note here the need to focus on relevant similarities and dissimilarities. For, strictly speaking, all analogies at some point break down. In our example, it would be false to suppose that humans and cows are exactly the same in all respects. However, the fact of some dissimilarities at all does not disprove the analogy. We must focus only on the properties that are relevant to the conclusion. In this example the conclusion is a moral claim about natural rights.

So, now we must ask: 'Which of these similarities and differences are relevant to the attribution of "natural rights" to both humans and cows?' Well, if you believe that the primary reason that humans have natural rights is the fact that they can suffer, then the fact that cows suffer is relevant and supports the analogy. On the other hand, you might say that our natural rights are specific to humans because we have some quality that cows do not have, such as the ability of rational thought. In this case, you would likely consider the vegetarian's argument to be an example of what is called *a false (or weak) analogy fallacy*. As you will see in the next chapter, a fallacy is an argument that contains an error in reasoning and that such arguments fall into different types.

Another way to critically evaluate an argument by analogy is to consider the supposedly uncontroversial claim. In this way, your critique of the analogy does not call into question the existence of relevant similar properties in the analogues. Rather, you are questioning whether or not those properties support the uncontroversial claim at all. In the argument above for the natural rights of cows, for example, you might argue against the claim that human beings possess natural rights. Some philosophers, for example, deny the existence of natural rights since there is little evidence for them. Therefore, if a capacity to suffer in humans does not support the claim to natural rights, then a cow's similar capacity would not support such claims.

Exercises

Instructions

For each of the following passages, identify the argument by analogy found within the passage and then critically evaluate the argument.

Passage 1

For the things we have to learn before we can do, we learn by doing, e.g. men become builders by building and lyre-players by playing the lyre; so too we become just by doing just acts, temperate by doing temperate acts, brave by doing brave acts.[1]

Passage 2

To me the question whether liberty is a good or a bad thing appears as irrational as the question whether fire is a good or a bad thing. It is both good and bad according to time, place, and circumstance, and a complete answer to the question, In what cases is liberty good and in what cases is it bad? would involve not merely a universal history of mankind, but a complete solution of the problems which such a history would offer.[2]

Passage 3

Consider the following example. Suppose there are twenty-six women and twenty-six men each wanting to be married. For each sex, all of that sex agree on the same ranking of the twenty-six members of the opposite sex in terms of desirability as marriage partners: call them A to Z and A' to Z', respectively, in decreasing preferential order. A and A' voluntarily choose to get married. Each preferring the other to any other partner. B would most prefer to marry A', and B' would most prefer to marry A, but by their choices A and A' have removed these options. When B and B' marry, their choices are not made nonvoluntary merely by the fact that there is something else they would each rather do . . . This contraction of the range of options continues down the line until we come to Z and Z' . . . Each prefers any one of the other twenty-five partners who by their choices have removed themselves from consideration by Z and Z'. Z and Z' voluntarily choose to marry each other. The fact that their only other alternative is (in their view) much worse . . . does not mean that they did not marry voluntarily . . . Similar considerations apply to market exchanges between workers and owners of capital. Z is faced with working or starving; the choices and actions of all other persons do not add up to providing Z with some other option . . . Does Z choose to work voluntarily? Z does choose to work voluntarily if the other individuals A thorough Y each acted voluntarily and within their rights.[3]

Passage 4

Questions about ends are, in other words, questions about what things are desirable. The utilitarian doctrine is that happiness is desirable as an end, and is the only thing that is so; anything else that is desirable is only desirable as means to that end. What should be required regarding this doctrine – what conditions must it fulfil – to justify its claim to be believed?

The only proof capable of being given that an object is visible is that people actually see it. The only proof that a sound is audible is that people hear it; and similarly with the other sources of our experience. In like manner, I apprehend, the sole evidence it is possible to produce that anything is desirable is that people do actually desire it.[4]

Passage 5

[I]nternational society as it exists today is a radically imperfect structure. As we experience it, that society might be likened to a defective building, founded on rights; its superstructure raised, like that of the state itself, through political conflict, cooperative activity, and commercial exchange; the whole thing shaky and unstable because it lacks the rivets of authority. It is like domestic society in that men and women live at peace within it (sometimes), determining the conditions of their own existence, negotiating and bargaining with their neighbours. It is unlike domestic society in that every conflict threatens the structure as a whole with collapse. Aggression challenges it directly and is much more dangerous than domestic crime, because there are no policemen. But that only means that the 'citizens' of international society must rely on themselves and on one another. Police powers are distributed among all the members. And these members have not done enough in the exercise of their powers if they merely contain the aggression or bring it to a speedy end – as if the police should stop a murderer after he has killed only one or two people and send him on his way . . . From this picture, two presumptions follow. The first . . . is the presumption in favour of military resistance once aggression has begun. Resistance is important so that rights can be maintained and future aggressors deterred. The theory of aggression restates the old doctrine of the just war: it explains when fighting is a crime and when it is permissible, perhaps even morally desirable. The victim of aggression fights in self-defence, but he isn't only defending himself, for aggression is a crime against society as a whole. He fights in its name and not only in his own. Other states can rightfully join the victim's resistance; their war has the same character as his own, which is to say, they are entitled not only to repel the attack but also to punish it. All resistance is also law enforcement. Hence the second presumption: when fighting breaks out, there must always be some state against which the law can and should be enforced. Someone must be responsible, for someone decided to break the peace of the society of states. No war, as medieval theologians explained, can be just on both sides.[5]

Passage 6

Look around the world: Contemplate the whole and every part of it: You will find it to be nothing but one great machine, subdivided into an infinite number of lesser machines . . . All these various machines, and even their most minute parts, are adjusted to each other with an accuracy, which ravishes into admiration all men, who have ever contemplated them. The curious adapting of means to ends exceeds the productions of human contrivance; of human design, thought, wisdom, and intelligence. Since, therefore the effects resemble each other, we are led to infer, by all the rules of analogy, that the causes also resemble; and that the Author of nature is somewhat similar to the mind of man; though possessed of much larger faculties, proportioned to the grandeur of the work, which he has executed.[6]

18 Informal fallacies

In Chapter 16, we discussed evaluating arguments and, in that chapter, we pointed out that an important task in evaluating arguments is determining whether an argument is logically correct. To recall, a logically correct argument is one in which the premises entail or provide probable support to the conclusion. In this chapter, we describe types of arguments that are not logically correct, that is, arguments in which the conclusion does not logically follow from the premises. When making arguments, we certainly wish to avoid faulty reasoning, but it is possible to make an argument that appears logically correct upon first glance, but actually contains a flaw in its logical reasoning. We call this sort of argument a fallacy. Whether we are evaluating someone else's argument or making one of our own, the ability to identify faulty reasoning is important. Without this ability, one might be tempted to accept the conclusions of arguments when there is no good reason to do so. In the end, as philosophers, we believe that our opinions should be grounded upon solid reasoning.

When an arguer commits a fallacy, it is often unintentional. Philosophers (and anyone else making an argument) usually do not set out to use faulty reasoning. So becoming familiar with some common fallacies will not only help you avoid using them in your own arguments, but will also help you identify them in the arguments of others. Fallacies come in two basic varieties: formal and informal. We will restrict our discussion to informal fallacies.

There are far more examples of fallacies than we have room to cover in this text, so we will restrict our discussion to the most common fallacies often committed by introductory philosophy students. These fallacies are: *ad hominem* (against the person), straw man, *petitio principii* (begging the question or circular reasoning), *ad ignorantium* (appeal to ignorance), *ad verecundiam* (appeal to inappropriate authority), *ad populum* (appeal to general belief), hasty generalization and false dilemma.

Ad hominem arguments mistakenly take aim at a person rather than at a position or argument. A person who employs this fallacy is often unable to respond in a good reasoned way to a position that he disagrees with. Consider this example: imagine that a Navy officer argues for the limited right of a state to resort to war by claiming that states, like individual persons, have the right to defend themselves against attack. A pacifist, attempting to argue against the officer, might commit an *ad hominem* fallacy by responding in the following way: 'we can't trust this officer's opinion because she is clearly a war monger; she is an officer in the Navy, after all.' Instead of attempting to provide a reasonable response to the argument itself, in other words, the arguer is merely attacking the Navy officer's character. Such an attack, however, does not provide a sound or cogent argument in defence of one's own position.

A *straw man* argument is similar to an *ad hominem* insofar as it involves a response to someone else's argument, but in this case, the arguer attacks a weakened or distorted view of the original argument. When responding to an argument, one ought to view it in its strongest form before arguing against it; failing to do so is an unjustified way to make your own argument appear stronger. This tactic is called the *straw man fallacy* since a straw man is easy to knock over. For example, imagine an opponent of evolution supporting her argument for biblical creationism by describing evolution as 'the simple idea that man is descended from monkeys'. Obviously, evolution is a theory that is far more complex than this unfair summary captures and is deserving of a more accurate representation. Thus, this opponent of evolution would be guilty of a straw man fallacy.

A *petitio principii* argument, otherwise known as begging the question or circular reasoning, is committed when the conclusion of an argument is assumed within one of the premises. One way an arguer might beg the question is by assuming the truth of a central claim, when such a claim is highly controversial. By assuming a controversial point that the opposing side does not accept as true, the arguer fails to provide a reasoned argument for the position itself. For example, an opponent of abortion might offer the following argument: 'murder is morally wrong, therefore, abortion is morally wrong'. This argument begs the question because it assumes the critical claim that all abortions are instances of murder. This claim is a controversial one that requires a reasoned argument, but by assuming its truth, the arguer skirts the issue. If everyone agreed that all abortions were murder, there would be far less controversy. Another way to beg the question is by assuming as a premise a claim that has the same meaning as the conclusion. For example, take this argument: 'men are better soldiers than women because men have more military skill than women'. One definition of soldier is someone who has military skill, so the argument can be restated, 'men make betters soldiers than women because they are better soldiers than women', which is clearly circular or begs the question.

An argument suffers from *ad ignorantium* (appeal to ignorance) when, instead of providing evidence in favour of a position, an arguer supports her own position by merely showing that the position has not been proven wrong. Philosophical argument, however, should focus on reasons for or against believing claims, not on historical or anthropological demonstrations of failed attempts to disprove the truth of claims. An example of this fallacy would involve arguments concerning the existence of aliens. The argument, for example, that 'since no one has proven that aliens do not exist, therefore they must exist' contains an *ad ignorantium* fallacy. Interestingly, someone could commit an *ad ignorantium* while arguing for the opposite claim that aliens do not exist. For example, the following argument commits this fallacy: 'since no one has proven that aliens exist, then they must not exist'.

An arguer commits an *ad verecundiam* (appeal to inappropriate authority) fallacy when she supports her position with the testimony of a person unqualified to provide expert knowledge on the given subject. Although we base a great deal of our knowledge on the testimony of others, doing so is intellectually legitimate only if the testimony comes from a person with the appropriate expertise. For example, we might hear a medical doctor, who is clearly an expert in medical matters, make a claim about evolutionary theory. In this case, the doctor's extensive knowledge of medicine and health does not grant him the legitimate authority to make an expert claim about evolution. Certainly, he is entitled to have a non-expert opinion on the matter, but it would be fallacious for someone else to cite his opinion as a way to argue for or against the theory of evolution.

A person is guilty of *ad populum* (appeal to general belief) when she provides evidence for the truth of a conclusion based on the general appeal of the belief. The fact that many (or even most) people believe something does not, by itself, prove the claim true. We can think of many examples that show this to be a fallacious form of reasoning. Studies show that approximately 85% of humans believe that there is a supernatural being or God; however, this is not a good reason to believe that God exists. There may be plenty of good reasons to do so, but this is not one of them.

An argument suffers from a *hasty generalization* fallacy when support for the conclusion is based on generalizations derived from insufficient data. The data used to support a claim must be grounded upon a sufficient number to make the conclusion likely. Consider this example: 'since three of my five college professors have been unfaithful to their spouses, most college professors must cheat on their spouses'. The evidence for this claim is not sufficient because the arguer has not investigated enough cases to properly represent the whole class of college professors.

A *false dilemma* fallacy is one in which the arguer stipulates that only two alternatives exist in a given situation when, in reality, there are more possibilities. For example, one might make the following fallacious argument:

1. All moral principles are universal or no moral principles are universal.
2. It is false that all moral principles are universal.

_____

3. Thus, there are no universal moral principles.

In the first premise the arguer ignores the legitimate possibility that some moral principles are universal while others are not. Some arguments legitimately rely on dilemmas that contain only two alternatives, but an argument is fallacious only if there are other possibilities available that the arguer does not consider.

Notice that all of these fallacies are similar in that they fail to provide an appropriate amount of evidence to support the claims being advanced. Just because an argument is fallacious does not mean that the conclusion is false, but it does mean that the logical foundation for the claim has not been established by the argument provided. Some fallacious arguments can seem convincing, too, given the set of beliefs that someone brings to the matter. We are more susceptible to be fooled by fallacious reasoning when the fallacious argument has a conclusion that we agree with. It is easier for us to overlook faulty reasoning when we agree with the conclusion, especially when the issue is an emotionally charged one such as abortion or the decision to go to war. Nevertheless, we ought to critically consider the logical basis of even the most cherished beliefs we hold in order to determine whether these beliefs are correct.

Exercises

Part A

Instructions
Identify the fallacy in each of the arguments below.

   *1. Most French citizens believe immigration laws are too lenient, therefore their immigration laws are too lenient.

   2. A recent National Rifleman's Association survey showed that 98 per cent of its members oppose gun control; therefore, most Americans oppose gun control.

   3. Either you support the death penalty or you support rape and murder. Since you don't support the death penalty, you must think rape and murder are morally permissible.

   4. My cousin has a Ph.D. in information technology, and she told me Toyota makes the most reliable hybrid cars these days. We may conclude that a Toyota Prius is the most reliable hybrid car.

   *5. Former US President Clinton is a draft-dodger, so we should ignore all of his opinions on international relations.

   6. People who oppose abortions do not respect women's right to choose. We should respect women's right to choose, thus we should support abortion rights.

7. God is the author of the *Bible*. I know this is true because the *Bible* states that God is the author.

8. Sony, a Japanese company, makes reliable audio equipment. Honda, the Japanese auto manufacturer, therefore likely produces reliable automobiles.

*9. You cannot prove to me that God does not exist. Thus, there's good reason to assume that He does.

10. The flat tax proposal says that everyone should be taxed according to the same rate. Obviously, this communist proposal is a bad idea since we can all see that communism is a corrupt political system.

Part B

Instructions

Take a side on each of the five subjects below and write an argument that is free of fallacies to support your side. Each argument should be approximately one paragraph in length.

1. The death penalty
2. The existence of God
3. Gun control
4. Abortion
5. Immigration reform

19 Finding arguments in philosophical texts

One of the main activities of philosophy is to present and defend arguments in support of one's claims. An argument, as we have seen, is a series of claims in which one of the claims (i.e., the conclusion) is said to follow from one or more of the other claims (i.e., the premises). To properly understand and evaluate a philosopher's arguments, then, it is necessary to recognize which of the author's claims are premises and which are conclusions. However, philosophers rarely lay out their arguments in *standard form* (see Chapter 14) with the premises and conclusions clearly identified. Instead, their arguments are often stretched out over long passages that contain much more than simply an argument. For example, philosophers might go off on tangents that are only indirectly related to their main argument, or they might provide examples to explain their views, or they might criticize opposing positions, or they might do any number of things that do not qualify as 'presenting an argument'. When reading a philosophical text, evaluation of the philosopher's claims is essential, but we must recognize philosophers' tendency to do much more than make arguments. Nevertheless, seeking to understand a philosopher's arguments is always a good place to start.

Ideally, claims are backed up by arguments. So, when you read philosophy you must be on the lookout not only for the author's claims, but also for the inferential relationship between the different claims being made. We must distinguish premises from conclusions, in other words, so that we can lay bare the inferences a philosopher draws between them. The following

exercises focus on the skill of identifying the premises and conclusions of arguments in the context of passages containing
additional and extraneous information. The skill involved, to
look at it another way, is the same skill as being able to identify
information that is not being used in an argument. It is important, in other words, to know what the author is arguing and
what she is not arguing.

In addition, the exercises will reinforce the skill learned in
Chapter 14, 'Understanding arguments'. As a reminder, once
you've identified the premises and conclusion of an argument in
a text, it is a good idea to put them into standard form. Recall
that an argument in standard form is one in which the premises
and conclusions are numbered in logical order and the conclusion
is separated from the premises by a line. For example, here is an
argument in standard form.

1. My idea of God did not arise from sense experience.
2. If my idea of God did not arise from sense experience, then
   it must be innate.

---

3. Thus, my idea of God is innate.

Exercise

Instructions
For each of the following passages, do these three things:

1. Identify (by underlining) the main conclusion of the
   passage.
2. Identify (by bracketing) any claims made in support of the
   conclusion.
3. Identify (by striking through) any sentences (or parts of
   sentences) that are not necessary to identifying the premises
   or conclusion of the argument.
4. Write out, in standard form, the main argument of the
   passage in your own words.

*Passage 1

Can you believe that there are people who call themselves Americans who think ownership of firearms is wrong? What kind of Americans do they think they are? The second amendment to the US *Constitution* establishes the right to bear arms. The *Constitution*, we should remember, is not only a legal document, but a moral one. Therefore, it is not wrong for US citizens to own a gun for personal use. We should send everyone who favours gun control to Mexico where they will wish they owned a gun.

Passage 2

Some consider school vouchers the way to improve the education of America's youth. Are they wrong? States should not adopt a school voucher system. According to a recent survey of public school teachers and administrators, school vouchers will destroy the American education system. Public schools are already operating in the red, so taking money from them to give to parents who want to send their children to private schools will surely be their ultimate downfall.

Passage 3

Although it may seem improbable to most football fans, the Bears are going to win the Super Bowl this year. They have not won a Super Bowl in over 25 years. The Bears have a storied tradition of overcoming adversity. This year the team had several fantastic first round draft picks that will surely give them an edge this season. Also, their coach has been making changes for the past few years that have made the Bears a much tougher team to beat. As long as the coach continues to make good coaching choices and the team does not suffer many significant injuries, then they are going to be donning the big rings in February.

Passage 4

Before we condemn others for the poor choices they make in life, we ought to consider whether humans are able to choose freely. It certainly seems true to us that we have free will; after all, isn't that one of the characteristics that distinguishes us from 'lower' animals? As unsettling as the idea that people don't have free will is, the empirical evidence is stacked against the idea of free will. There is a growing body of scientific evidence that seems to show that the rational decisions we make ultimately reduce to electro-chemical reactions in our brains. If our minds really are reducible to brains, then our choices are nothing more than physical reactions that are governed by physical laws. If this is true, then our minds (and therefore our choices) are also governed by physical laws that enslave those choices to events that are traceable back to the origin of the universe over which we have no control.

*Passage 5

When travelling to other countries, one of the aspects of those foreign lands you might notice is the fact that societies seem to have different moral standards. In some countries, a man may have more than one wife. Others have legalized prostitution or marijuana use. Some even allow for euthanizing the old. In our country, permitting these behaviours seems unthinkable to most. How could it be that there are so many moral principles that cultures disagree upon? The most reasonable explanation seems to be that there are no universal moral concepts or principles that apply to every culture. Therefore, moral absolutism is wrong and moral relativism is true.

Passage 6

A child cries from birth; the first part of his childhood is spent crying. At one time we bustle about, we caress him in order to pacify him; at another, we threaten him, we strike him in order to make him keep quiet. Either we do what pleases him, or we exact from him what pleases us. Either we submit to his whims, or we submit him to ours. No middle ground, he must give orders or receive them. Thus his first ideas are those of domination and servitude. Before knowing how to speak, he commands; before being able to act, he obeys.[1]

Passage 7

The history of science, like the history of all human ideas, is a history of irresponsible dreams, of obstinacy, and of error. But science is one of the very few human activities –perhaps the only one – in which errors are systematically criticized and fairly often, in time, corrected. This is why we can say that, in science, we often learn from our mistakes, and why we can speak clearly and sensibly about making progress there.[2]

Passage 8

Nothing can possibly be conceived in the world, or even out of it, which can be called good without qualification, except a good will. Intelligence, wit, judgment, and the other talents of mind, however they may be named, or courage, resoluteness, and perseverance as qualities of temperament, are undoubtedly good in many respects; but these gifts of nature may also become extremely bad and mischievous if the will which is to make use of them, and which, therefore, constitutes what is called character, is not good. It is the same with the gifts of fortune. Power, riches, honor, even health, and the general well-being and contentment with one's condition which is called happiness, inspire pride, and often presumption, if there is not a good will to correct the influence of these on the mind, and with this also to rectify the whole principle of acting, and adapt it to its end. The sight of a being who is not adorned with a single feature of a pure and good will, enjoying unbroken prosperity, can never give pleasure to an impartial rational spectator. Thus a good will appears to constitute the indispensable condition of even being worthy of happiness.[3]

Passage 9

[I]t is obvious to anyone who pays close attention that existence can no more be separated from God's essence than its having three angles equal to two right angles can be separated from the essence of a triangle, or than that the idea of a valley can be separated from the idea of a mountain. Thus it is no less contradictory to think of God (that is, a supremely perfect being) lacking existence (that is, lacking some perfection) than it is to think of a mountain without a valley . . . From the fact that I am unable to think of a mountain without a valley, it does not follow that a mountain or valley exists anywhere, but only that, whether they exist or not, a mountain and a valley are inseparable from one another. But from the fact that I cannot think of God except as existing, it follows that existence is inseparable from God, and that for this reason he really exists.[4]

Passage 10

As a challenge to theism, the problem of evil has traditionally been posed in the form of a dilemma: if God is perfectly loving, he must wish to abolish evil; and if he is all-powerful, he must be able to abolish evil. But evil exists; therefore God cannot be both omnipotent and perfectly loving. Certain solutions, which at once suggest themselves, have to be ruled out so far as the Judaic-Christian faith is concerned. To say, for example (with contemporary Christian Science), that evil is an illusion of the human mind is impossible within a religion based upon the stark realism of the Bible. Its pages faithfully reflect the characteristic mixture of good and evil in human experience. They record every kind of sorrow and suffering, every mode of man's inhumanity to man and of his painfully insecure existence in the world . . . There can be no doubt, then, that for biblical faith, evil is unambiguously evil, and stands in direct opposition to God's will.[5]

20 Reading a philosophical text in its historical context

The focus of the present exercise is a skill we call 'contextual reading', which involves reading a text within its historical and philosophical context. As mentioned in Chapter 2, reading philosophy can be a very challenging enterprise for a number of reasons. One of these reasons is often the historical gap between author and reader. Thus, a good place to start is to seek historical information concerning the author because it allows us to close that gap a little. While evaluating or criticizing philosophical arguments of others is a legitimate objective in philosophy, we must take care to understand these arguments as accurately and charitably as possible before engaging in this criticism. An important aspect of philosophers' arguments is the historical context in which they write.

The goal in the following exercise is to understand the text in a historical context so that you may gain a more accurate interpretation and deeper appreciation of the philosophical ideas entertained by the author. In other words, to have a deep and rich appreciation for an argument, you must do your best to understand what the author was arguing and why she was doing so. So before reading a primary text in philosophy, it helps to do some background research by seeking answers to such questions as:

- What were the historical circumstances in which the text was written?
- What goals might the author have had in writing this text?
- What are some of the author's central philosophical views and how do they relate to each other?
- Who might have been the author's intended audience?
- Is the text a response to other philosophical texts and, if so, which ones?

In addition to seeking out these answers, reading introductory material on the specific text itself is quite helpful. In many cases, primary texts include an introduction, written by a contemporary scholar with considerable knowledge of the primary text that offers a good overview of the text's main ideas. Introductory material may also be found in philosophy textbooks or, as is becoming more common, on websites devoted to philosophy. Two respectable websites for finding good overviews of philosophers and their ideas are the *Stanford Encyclopedia of Philosophy* and the *Internet Encyclopedia of Philosophy*. In any case, by finding out as much information about the historical and philosophical context of a particular text, you are better prepared to read and to more accurately interpret the text itself.

Exercise

Instructions

This exercise consists of a set of questions, an overview of a philosopher's life and philosophy, and a lengthy passage from a text by this philosopher. The philosopher in this case is Thomas Hobbes. The exercise prompts you to consider some background questions regarding a philosophical passage before reading the passage. You should be able to develop answers to these questions by reading the overview that precedes the philosophical passage. First, begin the exercise by reading the background questions. Second, read the overview and the philosophical passage. Finally, answer the questions at the end of the passage. The passage is entitled: 'Of Those Things That Weaken, or Tend to the Dissolution of the Commonwealth'.

Background questions

1. What were the main historical events of Thomas Hobbes's life?
2. Given the historical context, what do you think Hobbes's main goal was in writing *Leviathan*?
3. What are some of Hobbes's central philosophical views and how do they relate to each other?
4. Who might have been the intended audience of *Leviathan*?
5. Can you see Hobbes's text as an alternative to other philosophical positions with which you are familiar?

An overview of Hobbes's life and philosophy

Hobbes was born prematurely on 15 April 1588, in an English village called Westport. He jokingly blamed his mother's fear of the impending invasion of the *Spanish Armada* for his early arrival. Although the historical facts do not corroborate this explanation (the *Armada* set sail a month after his birth), there may be some truth to it since Hobbes's mother may have been frightened simply by rumours of an invasion. Hobbes's father, Thomas senior, was a minister of the Church of England who was fond of drinking and gambling. Thomas senior left his family behind, never to be seen again, when Hobbes was 16. In 1608, after finishing his formal education, Hobbes was hired by the aristocrat William Cavendish to tutor his son, also named William Cavendish. The connection with this family provided Hobbes with ample opportunities to meet important intellectuals all over Europe. On two occasions, for example, Hobbes accompanied a Cavendish on a European trip where he would have dealings with, among others, the scientist Galileo, the mathematician Marin Mersenne and the astronomer Pierre Gassendi. Starting late in his life, at the age of 40, Hobbes began an extended literary career covering such topics as political philosophy (for which he is most known), natural science, ethics, mathematics, history and translations of classical texts. After becoming seriously ill in 1679, Hobbes suffered a stroke and died within a week.

Hobbes divides his philosophical system into three branches, each of which studies a different kind of 'body': natural, human and political. *Natural philosophy*, Hobbes says, studies the fundamental properties of bodies in the natural world. This branch of philosophy includes physics, which investigates, for example, the motions of the stars and planets, the effects of gravity or the growth of plants and trees. In Hobbes's time, scientists such as Galileo were called 'natural philosophers' because they studied the natural world. Since natural philosophy uses both mathematics and geometry, it includes these sciences as well. Hobbes's natural philosophy is guided by the fundamental belief in *mechanistic materialism*, which, as the name suggests, claims that the universe is like a *machine* (i.e., a mechanism) and is composed only of *material* bodies. According to Hobbes, there are no spirits or souls, if these refer to incorporeal (non-physical) entities. Instead, the universe comprises only bodies that operate according to strict scientific laws of cause and effect. Every event, in other words, is caused by some other temporally prior event. The goal of natural philosophy is to understand the causes of physical motions by reducing all events and things to their fundamental motions. If we want to understand how a watch works, for example, we should take it apart and see how the parts interact.

The second branch of Hobbes's philosophy is *moral philosophy*, which specifically studies human bodies. Moral philosophy studies such aspects of our nature as our actions, emotions and states of mind. However, in keeping with his view of nature, Hobbes's description of these human properties or events is *mechanistic*. In other words, we are similar to machines, but machines with mental states and emotions. As Hobbes sees it, physical objects and events in the natural world start a series of internal 'motions' that ultimately cause not only our thoughts, but also our behaviour. So, for example, if a barking dog approaches me, I will become fearful, which will lead me to protect myself in some manner. The dog, in other words, causes fear in my mind, which, in turn, causes me to take action. Most human actions, if not all of them, Hobbes says, are motivated by the desire to achieve the 'good'. As Hobbes sees it, the individual desires of each person ultimately determine what is good or bad. For example, if I desire a piece of cake, the cake is 'good' to me. If another person wishes to avoid eating cake, then the cake is 'bad'. What is good or bad, in other words, is relative to each individual. There is no standard of goodness or badness that applies to all individuals. To put this another way, Hobbes adheres to what is called a *subjective notion of the good*. Hobbes is probably best known for his *pessimistic* depiction of the *state of nature*, a counterfactual state with no laws, legal enforcement or other aspects of organized society. In such a state, Hobbes argues, humans would be constantly at war with each other because individuals would selfishly seek their own good and not recognize any universal standards of behaviour. As such, the state of nature, he says, would be 'solitary, poor, nasty, brutish and short'.

The third branch of Hobbes's philosophy, *political philosophy*, deals with political bodies. In this branch of philosophy, Hobbes considers, among other things, the origin, maintenance and justification of political institutions. Hobbes's political views ought to be considered within their historical context. According to Hobbes, the serious political problems of his time resulted from disagreements over who has the ultimate authority in political and religious affairs. In 1626, around the time in which Hobbes likely started to develop the concepts of his future political theory, Charles I requested funds from Parliament to pursue war against Spain and France. Parliament denied Charles's request and he responded with a *Forced Loan*, by which he demanded individual subjects to loan him money. The unpopularity of this loan increased political tensions in England. The Forced Loan led directly to the Five Knight's Case, which itself magnified the political problems. The case started with the imprisonment of knights for refusing to pay the loan. The knights filed a Habeas Corpus suit and demanded that the King reveal the reason for their imprisonment. The King's attorney asserted that the knights were imprisoned *per special mandatum domini reges* (by special command of the King). This case raised important political questions about the limits of the King's right to command. Are the King's actions limited by the law? If so, does the King have the right to act outside of the law when circumstances require it? Answers to such questions exposed serious ideological differences between the King and Parliament that ultimately led to a civil war. Hobbes believed that political disagreements could be averted and peace firmly secured if his 'science of politics' could be adopted and followed by the sovereign power.

Hobbes found a methodological model for his political science in geometry. In the science of geometry, practitioners prove their conclusions on the basis of self-evident or commonly accepted principles. Hobbes, mimicking the method of geometry, attempts to ground his political argument on the 'obvious truth' of human behaviour (i.e., that humans are ultimately motivated to achieve their own good). If this truth is recognized, Hobbes believes, then conclusions may be drawn to which no rational person may disagree. The main conclusion of Hobbes's political philosophy is that peace in a commonwealth requires an *absolute sovereign power* that has the final say on all political and religious matters. An absolute sovereign would prevent conflict by creating laws and a system to enforce those laws. If people disobey the sovereign, Hobbes claims, they will ultimately return to a state of nature – a state that is beneficial to no one.

Passage

Though nothing can be immortal, which mortals make; yet, if men had the use of reason they pretend to, their commonwealths might be secured, at least from perishing by internal diseases. For by the nature of their institution, they are designed to live, as long as mankind, or as the laws of nature, or as justice itself, which gives them life. Therefore when they come to be dissolved, not by external violence, but intestine disorder, the fault is not in men, as they are the matter; but as they are the makers, and orderers of them. For men, as they become at least wary of irregular jostling, and hewing one another, and desire with all their hearts, to conform themselves into one firm and lasting edifice: so for want, both of the art of making fit laws, to square their actions by, and also of humility and patience, to suffer the rude and cumbersome points of their present greatness to be taken off, they cannot without the help of a very able architect, be compiled into any other than a crazy building, such as hardly lasting out of their own time, must assuredly fall upon the heads of their posterity.

Amongst the infirmities therefore of a commonwealth, I will reckon in the first place, those that arise from an imperfect institution, and resemble the diseases of a natural body, which proceed from a defectuous procreation.

Of which, this is one, *that a man to obtain a kingdom, is sometimes content with less power, than to the peace, and defence of the commonwealth is necessarily required.* From whence it cometh to pass, that when the exercise of the power laid by, is for the public safety to be resumed, it hath the resemblance of an unjust act; which disposeth great numbers of men, when occasion is presented, to rebel; in the same manner as the bodies of children, gotten by diseased parents, are subject to either untimely death, or to purge the ill quality, derived from their vicious conception, by breaking out into biles and scabs. And when kings deny themselves some such necessary power, it is not always, though sometimes, out of ignorance of what is necessary to the office they undertake; but many times out of a hope to recover the same again at their pleasure. Wherein they reason not well; because such as will hold them to their promises, shall be maintained against them by foreign commonwealths; who in order to the good of their own subjects let slip few occasions to weaken the estate of their neighbours.[1]

Questions

1. Knowing that Hobbes was writing in the context of a civil war, what does he mean by the following sentence?

   For men, as they become at least wary of irregular jostling, and hewing one another, and desire with all their hearts, to conform themselves into one firm and lasting edifice.

2. Based upon your knowledge of the historical circumstances, what is Hobbes's main goal in this passage?

3. In the overview you learned that the goal of natural philosophy is to understand the causes of physical motions. On the basis of this passage, in what way is Hobbes's political philosophy mimicking his method of natural philosophy?

4. Would your understanding of the following sentence change if Hobbes were writing specifically to a king rather than the citizens of a commonwealth? Why or why not?

   From whence it cometh to pass, that when the exercise of the power laid by, is for the public safety to be resumed, it hath the resemblance of an unjust act; which disposeth great numbers of men, when occasion is presented, to rebel.

5. Does *Leviathan* seem to be an alternative to other philosophical positions with which you are familiar?

21 Responding to essay prompts

As a student in a philosophy course, you will likely be required to write an essay in response to a prompt. Our experience reveals that students often fail to pay attention to the detailed instructions provided by instructors. Thus, we recommend that you read the essay assignment carefully, even though this might seem too obvious to mention. Ideally, the prompt will spell out all the information necessary for planning and executing the writing assignment. However, in some instances, your instructor might not provide you with a detailed, clear and/or informative prompt, in which case you ought to ask for assistance in acquiring the necessary information. In our opinion, there are four important components that should be included in writing prompts: purpose, audience, grading criteria, formal requirements.

Purpose. Your instructor ought to clearly explain the main purpose of the paper. There are a variety of ways that the purpose may be stated, but you will likely encounter such action terms as *summarize, defend, critically evaluate, analyze* or *criticize*. So, for example, you might be asked to 'summarize and critically assess Anslem's ontological argument' or to 'defend the morality (or immorality) of euthanasia'. Sometimes the question you have to answer is difficult to understand at first and requires a bit of reflection before proceeding. Make certain that you understand what is expected of you with regard to purpose and ask questions if the purpose is not clear.

Audience. The prompt should indicate the intended or imagined audience for your paper. Certainly, your instructor will likely be the actual audience, but that does not mean you should write an essay as if he is the only reader. The specification of an intended audience is meant to provide you with a target level for your paper. Are you expected to write at a level that is easily understood by your instructor or by an intelligent peer? If your instructor does not indicate an intended audience, it is worthwhile to ask.

Grading criteria. You should familiarize yourself with the instructor's grading criteria used to evaluate essays. Different instructors sometimes employ different criteria and assign different weights to the criteria. So, for example, some philosophy instructors believe that technical writing errors, such as spelling or grammatical mistakes, are highly unacceptable, while other instructors may look past a few mistakes and emphasize the philosophical arguments in the essay. If your instructor uses a grading rubric, use it to focus your efforts on the aspects of the assignment most emphasized by your instructor.

Formal requirements. Make sure you know and understand the formal requirements of the paper, such as due date, required length, documentation requirements and so on. Chances are, the instructor has put these requirements into the prompt because she considers them to be important. It is therefore prudent for you to consider them to be important too.

In some cases, your instructor will provide you with one topic, and you will have no choice but to address the required topic. In other cases, however, you may be allowed to devise your own topic or to choose one from a list. If you are required to choose a topic from a list, we suggest that you consider both your own interests and the difficulty level of the topic. Your motivation to write a strong essay will likely increase if you opt for a topic that is interesting to you. Also, despite an instructor's best efforts to avoid it, she may offer a list of essay topics that are of varying levels of difficulty. A prudent strategy is to ask your instructor whether challenging paper topics are graded in the same manner as easy ones. From our experience, students who choose difficult topics are given a certain amount of credit for taking on the harder task.

For introductory philosophy courses, it is unlikely that you will be asked to devise your own question for an essay assignment. According to some experts in college-level writing, good essay questions have three main characteristics; they are problematic, significant and interesting.[1] A *problematic* question is one in which a reasonable amount of controversy still exists. 'Does the earth revolve around the sun?' is not problematic in this sense, but 'What are the moral rights of the unborn?' is. To say a question is *significant* is to say that the question has meaningful consequences. 'Does God exist?' is a more *significant* question than 'Did God create the world in seven days?' Finally, a good question to pursue is one that is *interesting*, especially if it interests you as the writer. The following exercise will develop your ability to effectively respond to a philosophy essay prompt.

Exercises

Part A
Instructions
Read the following essay prompt and write out a list of questions that seek more clarification about the assignment.

Sample essay prompt

Assignment
In your essay, investigate three of the following ethical theories: divine command theory, utilitarianism, Kantian ethics, virtue ethics, natural rights theory. Furthermore, defend one of them as being the most reasonable.

Grading Criteria
Your essay will be scored according to standards of good writing.

Details
Essay Points: This assignment is worth 10 per cent of the course grade.

Due Date: 31 March.

Part B
Instructions
For each of the following questions, determine whether it would make a good essay question by stating whether it is problematic, significant and/or interesting.

⋆1. Is cigarette smoking morally wrong?
  2. Was the internment of Japanese-American civilians by the U. S. Government during World War II morally wrong?
  3. What is the nature of the human soul?
  4. Is the torture of animals morally wrong?
⋆5. Should we ignore scientific evidence when seeking the truth about reality?
  6. If a tree falls in a forest, does it make a sound?
  7. Can square circles exist?
  8. Under what conditions does a person deserve to be called 'tall'?
⋆9. Was Hitler a war criminal?
 10. Can we understand what it is like to think like a bat?

Part C

Instructions

Create your own list of problematic, significant and interesting questions that concern any philosophical issues discussed in your class (or from current events). If possible, compare your list with the lists of your colleagues.

Part D

Instructions

Spend a few minutes brainstorming on each of the 'good questions' in Part B.

Part E

Instructions

For each of the questions in Part B, write out a research plan. What kinds of information must you seek? Where would that information be available? How would you go about obtaining it?

22 Planning to write

Essay assignments in philosophy courses usually require that you attempt to justify your own beliefs about an issue, but they may also require you to evaluate the arguments given by others to justify their own opinions. Both of these tasks require that you be capable of developing and evaluating arguments (see Chapters 14–19). It is helpful when planning to write an essay that you discuss your ideas with others to help refine your position (see Chapter 4). Your paper should reflect the best articulation of your position, not your initial thinking on the subject. With this in mind, after receiving and reading an essay assignment, we recommend the following three steps as you begin the writing process: brainstorming, researching and outlining.

A brainstorming session may take different forms, but the main goal is the same: to allow your mind to run free with the topic without imposing too many restraints on your reflection process. For some, the best way to brainstorm is to free write on a piece of paper, that is, to just jot down all the thoughts that come to mind when one considers the topic. For others, brainstorming best occurs through conversation with others. In either case, when brainstorming, we recommend that you raise and attempt to answer some basic questions.

Brainstorming questions

1. What do I already know about this topic?
2. What is my opinion on this topic?
3. What led me to hold this opinion?
4. What arguments can be used to justify my opinion?
5. What arguments can be used to criticize my opinion?

6. Am I familiar with any philosophical ideas relevant to this topic?
7. What relevant facts do I need to find?
8. What do most people think about this topic?

After brainstorming, you should spend a reasonable amount of time conducting research. Research may take a variety of forms such as familiarizing yourself with the arguments on the subject, closely reading a particular philosopher's text or finding facts. For example, if you are writing an essay on the death penalty, it is probably important not only to find out the percentage of violent criminals who receive the death penalty each year or the average cost of a death penalty case, but also to read and understand philosophical arguments on both sides of the debate. In any event, a reasonable amount of time must be spent ensuring that you have all the necessary information needed to craft an effective and well-argued essay.

Outlining is also an important preparatory step in the writing process because it helps you organize and focus your thoughts into a coherent structure. Most philosophy essays follow a standard tripartite structure: introduction, body and conclusion. The introduction presents, among other things, the main claim or thesis of your essay (see Chapter 27 for more on introductions and conclusions). The body contains the important philosophical arguments on the topic. The conclusion summarizes the main claim of your essay, as well as points out a possible direction for future questioning. When outlining the essay, it is important to consider the main ideas to be developed in the body of the paper. The contents of the body will depend on the particulars of the essay assignment, but in many cases, it might contain a four-part structure: a detailed description of the topic, arguments for a particular claim, arguments against the claim and your position on the claim. An initial outline of a paper on the death penalty, for example, may look something like this:

- Introduction
- Body
    o Explanation of the death penalty
    o Arguments for the death penalty

o Arguments against the death penalty
o A statement and defence of my own position
- Conclusion

Using ideas generated from the brainstorming session and acquired by research, you ought to fill out the outline. For example, a more developed outline might look like this:

- Introduction
  o Background information about the death penalty
  o Why is this a significant question?
    □ People are being killed and this is important.
    □ Perhaps some of the people are innocent.
- Body
  o Explanation of the death penalty
    □ How many people are on death row?
    □ What crimes are subject to capital punishment?
    □ What's the financial burden?
  o Arguments for the death penalty (from philosopher X)
    □ Criminals deserve punishment.
    □ It deters others from committing bad crimes.
  o Arguments against the death penalty (from philosopher Y)
    □ It seems cruel and unusual.
    □ It might be racially biased.
    □ Eye for an eye' is unjust.
    □ Innocent people might be sentenced to death.
  o A statement and defence of my own position
    □ Support it.
    □ Why? I'm not sure yet.
- Conclusion
  o Restate my thesis and main arguments.
  o There may be possible questions to answer in future.

Keep in mind that a more detailed outline, such as the one above, is merely a starting point for the first draft of your essay. It is likely that new ideas will emerge after your writing is underway. Thus, it is important to be flexible and to be prepared to take a new direction if one is called for.

Exercises

Part A

Instructions

Brainstorm on the question 'Is it immoral to view pornography?' by free writing for 5–10 minutes. Use the questions stated in the chapter as a guide to your brainstorming session.

Part B

Instructions

On the basis of your brainstorming, write down a list of questions for you to pursue. Furthermore, list methods that you would use to find the answers to those questions.

Part C

Instructions

Imagine that you were assigned to write an essay that responds to the question of the morality of pornography. Write out a detailed outline. For each part of the outline, write a brief list of the ideas contained in that part.

23 Writing a descriptive essay

In Chapters 21 and 22, we discussed the preparatory steps for writing effective philosophical essays. We would like to emphasize here, however, that a requirement for good philosophical writing is a solid understanding and appreciation of the topic you will be writing about. The philosophical skills discussed previously that focus on critical thinking and reading are absolutely necessary to good writing. Good writing requires good thinking. So, unless you take the time to understand the issues and reflect upon them in a thoughtful, logical and rigorous manner, your philosophical writing will necessarily suffer. That being said, we will now turn our attention to the criteria of good essays so that you can learn not only how to write strong initial drafts, but also how to revise your essays into excellent pieces of writing.

Writing assignments in a philosophy course often require students to describe or evaluate (or both) a particular philosophical issue, text, position or argument. Descriptive essay prompts will use such words as *describe, summarize, explain, elaborate upon or demonstrate.* Evaluative essay prompts require one to do such things as *assess, criticize, defend, critically evaluate or examine.* In many cases, prompts involve both activities; for example, a prompt might ask a student to 'describe and criticize' or 'summarize and evaluate' a given philosophical topic. In this chapter, we focus on the criteria for good descriptive writing in philosophical essays. Of course, because philosophical essays are essays, the criteria for good writing in general will be identical to the criteria for good philosophical writing in particular. Thus, many of these criteria will also apply to essay writing in other courses and disciplines. In any case, a good descriptive essay does the following.

1. Presents an accurate and objective interpretation of the material. You should strive to present the material accurately and objectively, especially in cases where you will also present an evaluation. If you misrepresent a philosophical argument by presenting an inaccurate or biased description, your criticism will not be as effective and may even count as a *straw man fallacy*.

2. Indicates clearly, by use of attributive tags, that the ideas belong to someone else. An attributive tag is a phrase, such as 'Dr. Miller says' or 'According to Dr. Miller', that clearly indicates whose ideas are being described. In our experience, students often include their own ideas in a description without any indication. As such, it becomes difficult to determine which ideas belong to whom. We recommend that you not only use attributive tags often, but that you ensure to exclude your personal opinions from the description (even if you agree with the material described).

3. Focuses on the main ideas. Philosophers often address many issues at once, some of which may be tangential to the main arguments and claims. Good essays go to the heart of the matter and do not concern themselves with peripheral issues.

4. Describes the main ideas in an appropriate amount of space. If your essay prompt calls for description only, then the essay prompt should indicate the required length. In many cases, however, instructors will require you to evaluate a philosophical idea and not just describe it. In such cases, the descriptive portion functions as a summary that precedes the evaluation. As a good rule of thumb, summaries should be approximately 25 per cent of the paper's content, though you may wish to confirm this rule with your instructor.

5. Expresses ideas clearly and avoids unnecessary philosophical jargon. A common error in student writing is the failure to adequately paraphrase the ideas of another. It is important to be able to clearly express the ideas in your own words.

6. Uses and documents sources appropriately.

7. Avoids grammatical, punctuation and spelling errors.

Exercises

Part A

Instructions

Read the following passage by a philosopher named Ernst van den Haag and the three descriptive summaries of the passage. Then, answer the questions that follow the summaries.

Passage

In a recent survey Professors Hugo Adam Bedau and Michael Radelet found that 7,000 individuals were executed in the United States between 1900 and 1985 and that 25 of these individuals were innocent of capital crimes. Among the innocents they list Sacco and Vanzetti as well as Ethel and Julius Rosenberg. Although their data may be questionable, I do not doubt that, over a long period of time, miscarriages of justice will occur even in capital cases.

Despite precautions, nearly all human activities, such as construction or transportation, cost the lives of innocent bystanders. We do not give up these activities, because the advantages, moral or material, outweigh the unintended losses. Analogously, for those who think the death penalty just, miscarriages of justice are offset by the moral benefits and usefulness of doing justice. For those who think the death penalty unjust even when it does not miscarry, miscarriages can hardly be decisive.[1]

Summary 1

Philosopher Ernst van den Haag states that miscarriages of justice in capital punishment cases are inevitable, but that the benefits of the death penalty offset such miscarriages. He draws an analogy between those unjustly put to death by the justice system and those who die accidental deaths in other human activities. For those who consider the death penalty just, miscarriages of justice are unfortunate, but necessary. For those who consider the death penalty unjust, the small percentage of people mistakenly sentenced to death cannot really be used to launch a major strike against it.

Summary 2

Ernst van den Haag stupidly argues that although there are flaws in the death penalty, there is not enough evidence to abolish it. Twenty-five of the 7,000 people killed by the death penalty between 1900 and 1985 were innocent, but this percentage is tiny. Van den Haag lamely attempts to support his view by claiming that more people die each day performing routine activities, such as travelling to work, than all the innocent people killed by the death penalty in 85 years.

Summary 3

Philosopher Ernst van den Haag argues that the advantages of the death penalty, whether moral or material, outweigh the unintended miscarriages of justice. Despite precautions, van den Haag says, nearly all human activities, such as construction or transportation, cost the lives of innocent bystanders. He points out that we do not abandon these activities because the advantages outweigh the unintended losses. We accept, in other words, the deaths of innocent people when the benefits outweigh the costs. Similarly, he says, we should accept the death penalty.

Questions

Answer each question and briefly explain your answers.

    ★1. Which summary most accurately describes the ideas of the passage?
    2. Which summary is the least objective?
    3. Which summary uses attributive tags most effectively?
    4. Which summary captures all of the main ideas of the passage?
    ★5. Which summary is most clearly expressed?

Part B

Instructions

Read the following student description and circle words or phrases that indicate a lack of objectivity. Then, rewrite the passage to be more objective.

Student description

In 'Neo-Marxist Critique of Professional Sports', Stefano J. Glauser, who hasn't even played professional sports, defends the highly implausible Neo-Marxist view of competitive sports. Glauser rants that competitive sports not only reinforce the competitive nature of capitalist society, but also perpetuate false ideologies. For example, capitalists promote the ideology that says, 'if you work hard, you can achieve anything'. The fact of the matter, says Glauser, is that humans in capitalistic societies are fixed in their financial positions. In his unjustified opinion, there is very little upward mobility in our society. He actually wants us to believe that sports perpetuate this ideology by making people think success is possible and that hard work pays off. Yet, as he maintains, only a tiny fraction of people succeed in professional sports and for many, especially college football and basketball players, their hard work on the field reaps few financial rewards.

24 Paraphrasing philosophical texts

As discussed in Chapter 23, one characteristic of a good descriptive essay is that it provides an accurate and objective interpretation of a text or issue. We would like to offer a disclaimer here and mention that we believe objective and accurate interpretations of texts are generally possible. For a number of reasons, however, some philosophers call into question the ability to discover 'the meaning' of a text. First, language is often ambiguous and does not consistently convey one's intended message. Second, philosophers often deal with abstract concepts and ideas that are difficult to express in a precise and unequivocal manner. Third, readers of texts often approach them with different background assumptions and with different goals, each of which affect how they interpret the text.

Despite these difficulties, we believe it is possible to accurately interpret a text by properly understanding the point an author intended to make. The skill that we discuss in this chapter is paraphrasing a text. To paraphrase is to restate the ideas of a particular text or passage in one's own words. Accurate paraphrasing of a text is essential if you have been tasked with evaluating a philosophical position since you ought to present an accurate interpretation before criticizing it. Otherwise, you may be guilty of an error in reasoning known as the *straw man fallacy*. This chapter will break the skill of paraphrasing into three components: accuracy, use of one's own words and full representation of the essential elements of the original text or argument.

When paraphrasing a text, your first goal should be to accurately restate the author's ideas. Of course, this requires a proper understanding of the text itself, which may require you to refer to secondary texts in addition to the primary text in which you find the argument. Essentially, accurately restating someone else's argument means nothing more than representing the actual position that an author states in his writing.

Next, an effective paraphrase must capture all of and only the essential elements of the argument, that is, it must be complete. Rarely will you find a text that only includes essential elements of the author's argument, so you must strip away the nonessential portions in your paraphrase. You must take care not to omit those parts of the argument that are critical to providing justification for the ultimate conclusion of the argument. See Chapter 19 for advice regarding how to find an argument in a text.

However, your goal is not only to present an accurate and complete restatement of the author's ideas, but to show that you understand the ideas and state them in your own words. Therefore, you must try to avoid relying on the writer's specific words, grammatical structure or syntax. If you simply substitute synonyms from the original text, without changing the structure of the sentences, you are not demonstrating your grasp of the concepts. For example, in the following pair of sentences, the latter is not a good paraphrase of the former:

Euthanasia does violence to this natural goal of survival.[1]

Euthanasia does damage to this natural end of persistence.

Likewise, your true understanding is not revealed if you stick too closely to the terminology of the original source, even if you change the sentence structure. For example, the second sentence below sticks too closely to the terminology of the original text.

Euthanasia defeats these subtle mechanisms in a way that, in a particular case, disease and injury might not.[2]

These subtle mechanisms may be defeated by euthanasia in ways that even disease or injury might not.

To properly paraphrase, then, there needs to be substantial change in the terminology and structure of the original. For example, the second of each of these pairs makes a substantial change to the original:

Euthanasia does violence to this natural goal of survival.[3]

Euthanasia opposes our natural purpose to stay alive.

Or,

> *Euthanasia defeats these subtle mechanisms in a way that, in a particular case, disease and injury might not.*[4]

Euthanasia is unlike disease and injury insofar as the latter do not destroy these processes.

Exercise

Instructions

Each of the passages below is followed by a series of paraphrases of the main ideas of the passage. Choose the best paraphrase for each passage and explain the reasons for your choice.

---

*Passage 1

It might reasonably be expected in questions which have been canvassed and disputed with great eagerness, since the first origin of science and philosophy, that the meaning of all the terms, at least, should have been agreed upon among the disputants; and our enquiries, in the course of two thousand years, been able to pass from words to the true and real subject of the controversy.[5]

Paraphrases of Passage 1

1. It is reasonable to expect that many disputes in philosophy, since the first beginnings of science and philosophy, result from the failure to clearly define terms and that controversy has surrounded the words and not the true and real subjects of investigation.
2. We should expect philosophers to clearly define their terms if any progress is to be made in resolving a controversy.
3. One might have thought that previous philosophers would have clearly defined their terms so that philosophical discussion could focus on the substance of the issues and not just their terminology.

Passage 2

Liberty and Necessity are Consistent: As in the water, that hath not only liberty, but a necessity of descending by the Channel: so likewise in the Actions which men voluntarily doe; which (because they proceed from their will) proceed from liberty; and yet because every act of every man's will, and every desire, and inclination proceedeth from some cause, and that from another cause, which causes in a continuall chain (whose first link in the hand of God the first of all causes) proceed from necessity.[6]

Paraphrases of Passage 2

1. Humans make decisions freely, yet forces beyond their control ultimately determine these decisions.
2. Inanimate objects, such as rivers, have liberty.
3. There is nothing inconsistent concerning liberty and necessity.

Passage 3

Justice is a matter of not transgressing what the laws prescribe in whatever city you are a citizen of. A person would make the most advantage of justice for himself if he treated the laws as important in the presence of witnesses, and treated the decrees of nature as important when alone and with no witnesses present.[7]

Paraphrases of Passage 3

1. Being just is simply the act of adhering to the prescribed laws of the city you live in.
2. Justice is a matter of obeying the law, and a person has no good reason to abide by the law except when being observed by others.
3. Humans are naturally selfish and would do best if they observed the law only when in the company of others.

Passage 4

This problem is both the most difficult and the last to be solved by the human race. The difficulty (which the very idea of this problem clearly presents) is this: if he lives among others of his own species, man is an animal who needs a master. For he certainly abuses his freedom in relation to others of his own kind. And even though, as a rational creature, he desires a law to impose limits on the freedom of all, he is still misled by his self-seeking animal inclinations into exempting himself from the law where he can. He thus requires a master to break his self-will and force him to obey a universally valid will under which everyone can be free. But where is he to find such a master? Nowhere else but in the human species. But this master will also be an animal who needs a master. Thus while man may try as he will, it is hard to see how he can obtain for public justice a supreme authority which would itself be just, whether he seeks this authority in a single person or in a group of many persons selected for this purpose.[8]

Paraphrases of Passage 4

1. Humans are naturally unjust animals who need a master because, when granted a certain amount of freedom, they often abuse their freedom in relation to others of their own kind.
2. Government is necessary for humans to live in peace with each other.
3. It is difficult to establish a just government because humans are selfish by nature and will avoid obeying the law whenever possible.

*Passage 5

[Although] God could not have known what Adam and Eve, or Satan, would do if he created them, he could surely know what they might do . . . If so, he was taking, literally, a hell of a risk when he created Adam and Eve, no less than when he created Satan. Was the freedom to make unforeseeable choices so great a good that it outweighed the risk?[9]

Paraphrases of Passage 5

1. Was God's decision to give human beings the freedom to make decisions for themselves a bad one?
2. Is God ultimately responsible for the evil that results from human decisions and actions?
3. Does the good of human freedom outweigh the bad that results from it?

25 Writing an evaluative essay

In Chapter 23, we addressed the criteria of good descriptive essays. This chapter explains the characteristics of good evaluative essays. Evaluative essay prompts might ask you to do such things as *evaluate, discuss, criticize or assess*. As previously mentioned, some essay assignments will require you to do both, that is, describe and evaluate a particular philosophical issue. The key difference between descriptive writing and evaluative writing is that while the former is aimed at presenting an objective account, the latter presents a critical approach to the issues.

Expressing an effective, interesting and insightful evaluation of a philosopher's position in essay form is one of the cornerstones of being able to do philosophy. To write an essay that contains an effective and well-developed critical evaluation, you need to do some preparatory reading, thinking and discussing. This preparatory work comprises mastery of many of the skills previously addressed in this book. In other words, to successfully write an evaluative essay, you ought to carefully read the philosophical text (Chapters 2, 19 and 20), identify and evaluate the philosophical claims (Chapters 12 and 13), identify and evaluate the arguments (Chapters 14 to 16) and present an accurate and objective description (Chapters 23 and 24).

The products of doing these activities will give you the building blocks of a good evaluative essay. However, one of the hallmarks of a good evaluation is an ability to focus your essay around *your own* argument and central claim. This is the key feature that distinguishes an evaluative essay from a descriptive essay – your evaluation should seek to make an argument about the philosopher or philosophical position at issue. When evaluating a philosophical position, you do not need to summarize or discuss every claim, argument or observation made by one who holds the position in question. Rather, you need only address the claims of the position insofar as they are relevant to your argument and are necessary to present the position fairly.

Once you have done all the preparatory thinking, you should be able to write a good critical evaluation that makes an argument consistent with any (or all) of the following strategies:

1. Points out that one or more important claims are problematic (i.e., false, unsupported or implicitly assumed). As we have seen in Chapter 8, claims ought to be clear, consistent, compelling and supported with good arguments.
2. Identifies logical flaw(s) present in the inferences of the argument you are evaluating. In Chapter 14, we have seen that a good argument is *logically correct*, that is, the conclusion necessarily or probably follows from the premises.
3. Shows how the central claims or extended arguments do not follow from the supporting arguments or are subject to a possible counter-example or argument.
4. Draws out interesting consequences from an argument (such consequences could count in favour of or against the argument in question).

While the strategies above are by no means exhaustive, they are a good way to help get your evaluation started and off the ground. Whichever strategy you settle on, you should always write in a manner that is consistent with the requirement to be clear. That is, you ought to present your argument explicitly by avoiding philosophical jargon, arguing in the first person and describing the inferences your evaluation seeks to make. Your thinking must account for the required length of the essay. Very often, students take on too much in short essays and end up either writing an incomplete argument or an overly broad one.

Note that the following exercise contains sample evaluations that are shorter than you might actually find in a student essay. Despite this fact, you should still be able to get a sense of the principles at work. However, actual evaluative essays and arguments are usually longer.

Exercise

Instructions

Read the following passage by a philosopher named J. Gay-Williams, the evaluations of the passage and then answer the questions that follow.

Passage

Every human being has a natural inclination to continue living. Our reflexes and responses fit us to fight attackers, flee wild animals, and dodge out of the way of trucks. In our daily lives we exercise the caution and care necessary to protect ourselves. Our bodies are similarly structured for survival right down to the molecular level. When we are cut, our capillaries seal shut, our blood clots, and fibrogen is produced to start the process of healing. When we are invaded by bacteria, antibodies are produced to fight against the alien organisms, and their remains are swept out of the body by special cells designed for clean-up work.

Euthanasia does violence to this natural goal of survival. It is literally acting against nature because all of the processes of nature are bent towards the end of bodily survival . . . It is enough, I believe, to recognize that the organization of the human body and our patterns of behavioral responses make the continuation of life a natural goal. By reason alone, then, we can recognize that euthanasia sets us against our own nature. Furthermore, in doing so, euthanasia does violence to our dignity. Our dignity comes from seeking our ends. When one of our goals is survival, and our actions are taken to eliminate that goal, then our natural dignity suffers. Unlike animals, we are conscious through reason of our nature and our ends. Euthanasia involves acting as if this dual nature – inclination towards survival and awareness of this as an end – did not exist. Thus, euthanasia denies our basic human character and requires that we regard ourselves or others as something less than fully human.[1]

Evaluations of the passage

Evaluation 1

The author is guilty of a logical error when he tries to derive an 'ought' from an 'is'. By this, I mean that he is claiming that our nature 'ought' to be what it 'is'. Nature, in other words, has given us a desire for survival so we ought to try to survive. Yet, just because we have this desire does not mean that we should have it or that we should act upon it. Sometimes, I get naturally angry at other drivers, and I feel like I want to drive my car into theirs. If I allowed nature to be my guide in such a situation, I would likely do something that is harmful and even immoral. It seems that acting against my nature, in this situation, is the right thing to do. The author concludes that we should not practice euthanasia, but this does not follow from the fact that euthanasia works against our nature.

Evaluation 2

J. Gay-Williams' argument against euthanasia runs into a number of problems. First, his argument relies on the highly questionable claim that 'our dignity comes from seeking our ends'. Contrary to his claim, one might reasonably believe that our dignity comes from the fact that we are autonomous agents responsible for imposing moral laws upon ourselves. Second, Gay-Williams assumes that our natural bodily processes, such as blood clotting, indicate that 'survival' is a natural telos for humans. But does this mean that any type of survival is always a natural end for us? A soldier, for example, might decide to sacrifice himself for the good of his fellow troops during a particular battle. Assuming that the situation calls for such a sacrifice, the soldier would be doing the morally appropriate action acting contrary to nature and against his natural end. Clinging to life in certain circumstances is not a manifestation of dignity. Thus, Gay-Williams needs to show that survival in the face of an incurable disease leading to an imminent and painful death is a dignified choice. A final criticism is that he assumes that nature provides a moral guide to ethical conduct. Nature, however, does not always point us in the right direction. For these reasons, Gay-Williams' argument is not a good one.

Evaluation 3

The author of the passage, J. Gay-Williams, fails to write a persuasive argument against euthanasia. He makes a handful of scientific claims that are backed without any proof whatsoever. He also claims to know what human nature is, but this is a deep philosophical puzzle that has no definitive answers. He is also guilty of a fallacy of composition. Philosophical arguments require logical correctness and truth. Unfortunately, Gay-Williams provides neither of these in his argument against euthanasia, leaving the reader to wonder. Furthermore, he writes with an attitude of authority on matters in which he has not established his credentials.

Questions

Rank the critical evaluations in order from best to worst in their effectiveness in each of the five areas below. Also, explain your rankings.

*1. Exposing false, unsupported or questionable claims.
2. Exposing logical flaw(s) in Gay-Williams' argument.
3. Focusing on main claims and arguments.
4. Developing the evaluative ideas.
5. Clearly expressing the ideas without unnecessary philosophical jargon.

26 Using quotations effectively

Philosophical questions, given the fact that they are both central to human existence and difficult to definitively answer, have a long history. In order to properly address philosophical questions, then, you will often need to address the work of prior philosophers, and this may include the need to directly quote from these philosophers. However, using someone else's words is something you ought to do sparingly, and only when you have a specific purpose in mind because the focus of your writing should normally be your own analysis of a philosophical topic (unless, of course, you are assigned to write a summary essay). So, in order to use quotations effectively, we recommend two things: (1) use quotations for the right reasons, and (2) incorporate them properly into your own writing.

Good reasons to use quotations

1. To support your own argument by relying on a legitimate authority.
2. To show that your description is accurate (or justified).
3. To add style or flair to your paper because the original text is beautifully written and powerful.
4. To communicate the author's idea more effectively than a paraphrase of the idea.
5. To do a careful analysis of a philosopher's position.

Once you have decided that there is a specific need to use a quotation, you should ensure that you incorporate it into your own writing properly. Below are suggestions you should follow when using quotations:

1. Author introduction: explain why the author, whose words you are quoting, is relevant to your discussion.
2. Context: rather than quoting a long portion of the author's work to provide context, use your own words to do so.
3. Paraphrase after quotation: assume that your reader will not interpret the quotation the same way you do, so show her how you understand it.
4. Block quotation: set long quotations (usually three full lines or longer) off from the rest of your essay by indention and single spacing. Consult your instructor for specific guidance. Use block quotes infrequently.
5. Inserted sentences (complete sentences): start an inserted complete sentence with a capital letter, separated by comma from introductory phrase. For example, 'Quote this'.
6. Inserted phrases (incomplete sentences): work phrases into the natural grammatical structure of your sentence. Sometimes you may need to add, delete or modify parts of the phrase. Use an ellipsis (. . .) when you delete words. Use brackets when you add or modify words.
7. Precision: use exact words from the text when the grammatical structure allows it.
8. Documentation: consult your instructor for specific documentation requirements.
9. Do not use quotations merely as a way to meet a minimum word count.

Exercises

Part A

Instructions

Read Passage 1 below from the article entitled 'A defense of abortion' by Judith Jarvis Thomson and answer the questions that follow.

Passage 1

Suppose you find yourself trapped in a tiny house with a growing child. I mean a very tiny house, and a rapidly growing child – you are already up against the wall of the house and in a few minutes you'll be crushed to death. The child on the other hand won't be crushed to death; if nothing is done to stop him from growing he'll be hurt, but in the end he'll simply burst open the house and walk out a free man. Now I could well understand it if a bystander were to say, 'There's nothing we can do for you. We cannot choose between your life and his, we cannot be the ones to decide who is to live, we cannot intervene'. But it cannot be concluded that you too can do nothing, that you cannot attack it to save your life. However innocent the child may be, you do not have to wait passively while it crushes you to death. Perhaps a pregnant woman is vaguely felt to have the status of a house, to which we don't allow the right of self-defense. But if the woman houses the child, it should be remembered that she is a person who houses it.'

Questions

> *1. Summarize, in a few sentences, the main ideas of Passage 1. In your summary, be sure to incorporate exactly one sentence from the passage.
> 2. Explain the reasoning behind your choice in Question 1.
> 3. Underline 3-4 consecutive sentences in the above passage that best encapsulates the main idea. Explain your answer.

Part B

Instructions

Read the following passage from Richard Rorty's *Achieving Our Country* and then evaluate the use of quotations in the numbered statements following the passage. Imagine that the statements are taken from student papers on the passage. The two main questions to use in your evaluation are: Is the choice of quotation a good one? Is it properly formatted?

Passage 2

The reformist American Left of the first two-thirds of the century accomplished a lot. But most of the direct beneficiaries of its initiatives were white males. After women won the right to vote, the male reformers pretty much forgot about them for forty years. Right up through the early Sixties, male leftists in the hiring halls and faculty lounges often spoke of women with the same jocular contempt, as did male rightists in the country clubs. The situation of African-Americans was deplored, but not changed, by this predominantly white Left. The Democratic Party depended on the Solid South, and Franklin D. Roosevelt had no intention of alienating Southern white voters in order to help blacks. Trade union leaders like the Reuther brothers, who desperately wanted to integrate the unions, could not do much to diminish racial prejudice among the rank and file.[2]

Student Statements

★1. According to Rorty, the Left in America 'accomplished a lot' in the first part of the twentieth century.

2. Franklin D. Roosevelt, Richard Rorty asserts: 'had no intention of alienating Southern white voters in order to help blacks'.

3. Even trade unions, 'could not diminish racial prejudice among rank and file.'

4. The situation Rorty describes is not much different today since even now 'male leftists in the hiring halls and faculty lounges often spoke of women with the same jocular contempt'.

5. Richard Rorty points out that the Leftists in America accomplished a great deal of social progress in the first part of the twentieth century.

The Democratic Party depended on the Solid South, and Franklin D. Roosevelt had no intention of alienating Southern white voters in order to help blacks. Trade union leaders like the Reuther brothers, who desperately wanted to integrate the unions, could not do much to diminish racial prejudice among the rank and file.

27 Writing effective introductions and conclusions

The introduction and conclusion are very important parts of your essay because they establish and reinforce your argument in the mind of the reader. Our suggestions in this chapter are based on the assumption that you are writing a thesis-driven essay. Good introductions of thesis-driven essays establish your argument by accomplishing two objectives: (1) offering a clear thesis statement that helps focus the essay by stating a specific and clearly defined philosophical claim; and (2) providing contextual information for a proper appreciation of the philosophical issue you are investigating. We also believe that introductions should provide a roadmap of the essay, though such a roadmap is not necessarily required. Effective conclusions reinforce and close your argument for the reader by doing two things: (1) restating the main evidence and inferences that support your thesis; and (2) acknowledging possible weaknesses in your argument or possible avenues for future investigation.

A central feature to both introductions and conclusions is the thesis statement. A strong thesis in a philosophical essay states a claim that is clear and thought-provoking. It is important to include the thesis statement in the introduction to frame the reader's mind and to specify your intentions up front. Also, there are a few rules of thumb to help ensure a strong thesis. First, you should write your thesis, and your philosophy essay in general, in the first person with personal pronouns. That is, an acceptable way to start a philosophy paper is with the words, 'In this paper I will argue that . . . ,' though you might save such a sentence for the end of the introduction. Second, your thesis should be able to answer why or how your central claim answers the question at hand. For an assignment about the justification of killing, an example of a good first sentence might be, 'In this paper I will argue that it is morally permissible to kill in self-defence because such acts accord with our intuitions about the value of human life'. Finally, as always, write your thesis in clear, simple language.

For some students these suggestions may seem strange. Students often feel the need to 'hook the reader' with a claim that indicates the importance of the subject matter. Also, students new to philosophy often try to write in profound or technical language because they believe such language is called for. However, attempts to fascinate the reader often result in confusing sentences, awkward writing and false claims. Be especially cautious of the common mistake of opening your essay with what we call a 'dawn of time' statement. For example, if you were writing an essay on the moral justification for killing human beings, you should not start with a sentence of the sort: 'People in many cultures and throughout history have debated about when it is permissible to kill another human being'. Such claims are vague and difficult to support with evidence. Students who use 'dawn of time' statements are often trying to do the right thing, which is to provide a context for the reader, but do so in the wrong way. This leads to another important point about introductions, namely, that they should provide a certain amount of background information to set up the main thesis. However, what kind and how much information is necessary for providing a context depends on your intended audience.

After providing contextual information and presenting a strong thesis, a good introductory paragraph could also walk the reader through a sketch, or roadmap, of your argument that supports your thesis. It is important to note here that your thesis should demonstrate why your claim answers the question at hand since your argument will demonstrate why your claim, after analysis, is compelling. So, the rest of your introduction should present in an abbreviated form the basic tracks of your argument. Tell the reader, in explicit detail, what each step of your argument will be and why you are taking that step. By the end of your introduction, the reader should be able to clearly understand your central claim and how you intend to argue for that claim. In short, the introduction might offer a basic structure of the body of your argument and, therefore, an outline of your whole paper.

Your conclusion should represent your work in summary form. It is important to do this in the same logical order as you did in the introduction. Here you are simply recounting for the reader the steps of your argument and how those steps support your thesis. If you stay focused on your thesis, you will refresh the reader's understanding of the main points of your argument while simultaneously avoiding common errors in writing essay conclusions. Too often, students writing philosophy include new and un-established claims in their conclusions. Even if such claims are related to the thesis, introducing new ideas distracts your reader and leaves him expecting an argument for these new claims. Also, students sometimes overstate the strength of their thesis; doing so makes the author appear foolish and naïve. A good summary paragraph, by staying within the scope of your argument, will indicate the need for further investigation and interesting conceptual relationships without overstating the strength of the claims or introducing a new idea.

Finally, we suggest that you close your argument in a way that recalls your thesis to the mind of the reader. Using your thesis to 'bookend' your paper is a clear and effective way to communicate with your reader. The introduction and conclusion of your paper are important because they can deliver your thesis, in clear and explicit terms, to the mind of the reader.

Exercises

Part A

Instructions

Rank the following three introductions in terms of their effectiveness. Furthermore, explain and justify your rankings. Assume that these are introductions to a student essay that is supposed to describe and critically evaluate an argument for capital punishment by an author named Ernst van den Haag.

Student introductions

Introduction 1

Since the beginning of the establishment of capital punishment, a raging and heated debate has ensued over its moral status. Is it ethically right to kill another person even in cases where that person is responsible for the murder of another? On the one hand, some have claimed that it is a morally despicable act carried out under the guise of governmental legitimacy. On the other hand, some argue it is a perfectly ethical form of punishment. Where do you stand on this important social and ethical issue? Haag stands on the side of the death penalty when he responds to the arguments of the abolitionists who oppose the death penalty. His arguments, however, are not valid and his case for capital punishment is therefore quite weak.

Introduction 2

In his essay, 'The ultimate punishment: A defense', Ernst van den Haag argues for the preservation of the death penalty. In making his argument, van den Haag addresses and refutes several points commonly made by abolitionists, that is, those who would like to abolish the death penalty. Van den Haag's main point is that the death penalty is a just punishment and that justice itself overrides all other factors concerning capital punishment. In this paper, I summarize and provide a critical evaluation of van den Haag's argument. I shall argue that van den Haag's argument does not take into consideration the true value of human life and, for that reason, his argument ultimately fails.

Introduction 3

The death penalty was first recorded in the United States in 1608, when Captain George Kendall was convicted of being a spy for Spain and was executed in Virginia's Jamestown colony. Since that time, a large number of people have been put to death in America at the hands of the U. S. justice system. But we must ask: 'Is such a practice a moral one?' Some philosophers have attempted to answer this question. One such person is Ernst van den Haag, a Dutch-American professor of jurisprudence, who lived from 1914 to 2002 and taught at Fordham University. While he lived, he was a good friend of the conservative political analyst

William F. Buckley. According to van den Haag, the death penalty is a completely justified punishment for heinous crimes such as murder and torture. His argument, which will be described and critically evaluated within this essay, contains a number of false assumptions and invalid inferences.

Part B
Instructions

Rank the following three conclusions in terms of their effectiveness. Furthermore, explain and justify your rankings. Assume that these are conclusions to a student essay that is supposed to describe and critically evaluate Ernst van den Haag's argument for capital punishment.

Student conclusions

Conclusion 1
Both of Ernst van den Haag's arguments against the death penalty have been shown to be weak for one reason or another. His argument for the conclusion that the financial cost of capital punishment cases is irrelevant to determining its morality does not account for that fact that the allocation of public resources is an ethical matter. Similarly, his argument that claims the death penalty is not cruel and unusual requires the acceptance of highly questionable assumptions. Although his arguments are weak, it should be noted that I have not advanced any arguments against capital punishment. Such arguments, although important to make, are beyond the scope of this paper and must await another day for proper airing.

Conclusion 2
Capital punishment, as we have seen, is an important issue that should not be taken lightly. Unfortunately, the poor arguments offered by Ernst van den Haag provide good evidence for the claim that he does not consider the issue with the gravity required. Philosophical issues, especially ethical ones, demand a constant questioning of our assumptions and foundational beliefs. When people rely simply on gut instincts, as van den Haag does in his

arguments, we have a recipe for disaster. The crafting of laws must be done with the help of a moral compass and when our lawmakers accept arguments such as van den Haag's, then we can expect the passage of any number of bad laws with bad consequences. It is important that we prevent, or overturn, such terrible legal practices as capital punishment.

Conclusion 3

In this essay, I described and evaluated two arguments in favour of the death penalty by a professor of jurisprudence named Ernst van den Haag. I looked at both arguments from a perspective of logic. In both cases, van den Haag's arguments were shown to be problematic. The first argument, as we have seen, contained two false premises. The second argument was not logically correct because its premises did not support its conclusion. Thus, his arguments in favour of the death penalty were shown to be poor.

Part C

Instructions

Using the information contained in the above introductions and conclusions, write your own introduction and conclusion to the imagined essay assignment. (Note: since you are probably not familiar with the specific ideas, assume that the information in the introductions and conclusions is correct.)

28 Revising an essay

A good way to think about writing, whether philosophical or otherwise, is to consider it a process, not a discreet event in time. The most effective writers are the ones who return repeatedly to their work to find ways to improve it. Ideally, you will have an opportunity to *revise* your draft philosophical essay. The word *revise* is derived from the Latin word *revisere*, which means 'to see again' or 'to visit again'. Bearing this in mind, we recommend that you think of the practice of revision not simply as a manner of correcting mistakes, but as a way of reconsidering the essay's ideas and structure by 'seeing it with fresh eyes'. In some cases, your instructor will require you to revise your essay in response to some of her feedback. In other cases, however, you will be responsible for turning in a final draft without the benefit of your instructor's comments. In such cases, we urge you to finish your draft with enough time to allow willing peers to read and respond to the draft. Furthermore, allowing yourself to get some 'distance' from your essay is a good way to find aspects to improve. In other words, let your essay sit for a number of days before you revise it.

When you revise your essay, you should first think of revision in terms of what some writing experts call *global revision*, in contrast to *local revision*.[1] Global revision involves major changes and additions to your essay, and it focuses on the force and organization of the ideas themselves. When you revise globally, you will find yourself moving whole paragraphs, scrapping large passages and rewriting them, or adding long examples or explanations of ideas. Local revision, on the other hand, is the process of paragraph and sentence-level editing where you do such things as identify and correct grammatical and spelling errors, improve style and sentence flow or ensure that paragraphs are unified around a central claim. While both types of revision are necessary, we have found that students often fail to take seriously the idea of global revision, so we will start at this level.

To perform a global revision effectively, it is important to look again at the main ideas of your essay to ensure you have clearly presented the ideas and sufficiently provided support in an organized way. A good starting point for global revision is for you to ask yourself the following questions:

- What is my thesis, and have I stated it clearly?
- Can the reader easily identify the evidence supporting the thesis?
- Does the evidence actually support the thesis?
- Does the essay follow a logical organization?

In short, these questions ask whether you have clearly articulated and offered good arguments in support of your main claims (see Chapters 11 and 20).

Once you are satisfied with the answers to the above questions, you can begin to move from a global to a local perspective. We can further break down local revision to two levels: paragraph and sentence. Consider paragraph-local revision first. Each paragraph of your essay should focus on a single main idea or concept, and all of the sentences in that paragraph should provide support or elaboration for that idea. Support and elaboration for the main idea can include particular examples, facts or theories. To ensure that paragraphs have this unity, it is helpful to raise and answer the following questions about each paragraph:

- What is its main point?
- Why is this paragraph important to the whole essay?
- Have I supported the main idea with relevant particulars?
- Does each sentence of this paragraph play a relevant role in explaining or supporting the main idea?

In cases where such questions are difficult to answer, you should revise your essay at the paragraph level.

Finally, you should turn your attention to sentence-level local revision only after you confirm that you have clearly stated the main ideas of your essay and have adequately supported and organized them in a logical sequence. With local revision at the sentence level, you can use the following questions as a guide:

- Is every sentence clear and informative?
- Is every sentence necessary to the argument?
- Are there any awkward and/or wordy sentences?
- Should I change any particular words for the sake of clarity, style or philosophical precision?
- Is the essay free of grammatical, spelling and punctuation errors?

After doing a final revision of the essay, you should ensure that you have documented and formatted your essay according to the requirements of the essay prompt.

Exercises

Part A

Instructions

Read the following student passage and the accompanying questions. Imagine that the essay is supposed to be between 500 and 700 words and is written in response to the following: 'Is it reasonable to believe in God? Why or why not? Defend your answer'.

Student passage

A never-ending argument in society is the argument concerning God's existence. Since the beginning of human history, both sides of this debate have given sound arguments in defence of their views, but which is more reasonable, one might ask. Did an omnipotent being create and control the universe? Or, is it just a matter of dumb luck that we exist at all? An examination of the arguments on both sides of this debate will yield fruitful results. Can we know for sure? At this point, we might not have an answer to this question.

There are many things and events that happen in this world about which we have no idea what their cause is. For example, we cannot really explain where gravity comes from nor can we explain how a person miraculously recovers from a life-threatening illness. It is because of these unanswerable questions that it is reasonable to believe in God.

Also, if we take the time to observe the world and the things and events in it, it is hard to deny that God exists. The complexity of the design of the world is the proof that there is a God. In fact, human beings themselves are proof of an omnipotent and benevolent designer/creator. According to a philosopher named William Paley, the complexity of the world proves that God exists because how could the world be so complex by chance? Paley analogizes the world to a watch. If you found a watch while walking along the beach, you would recognize that it could not have simply appeared there by chance. Instead, you would say that the watch requires a watchmaker. Likewise, when you see the organization and apparent design of the world, you must conclude that there is a designer. So if humans, who are finite and intelligent beings, can create watches but not the world, then there must be an infinite being who is responsible for creating the world.

Every effect in the world has a cause. If you look at the world around you, it is obvious that each event has been caused. The rain causes grass to grow, gravity causes rocks to fall and water crashing down a waterfall causes a sound. All of this shows evidence of design.

To believe in God is clearly more reasonable than to doubt the existence of God. If we doubted the existence of God, we would not be able to explain the complex design of the universe. Nature itself does not have the power of thought. It cannot rationally solve a problem. Humans, however, can do both. Despite this fact, we cannot come close to designing something as complicated as the world, or even a human eye. It is not logical to believe that such design could come about by pure chance and blind scientific laws. The best answer is God.

Questions

Global revision questions

1. How would you state the thesis of this essay?
2. Is the thesis clearly stated?
3. What evidence or reasons are offered to support the thesis?

4. Is the thesis supported well?

5. What additional information, if any, could help the author better support the thesis?

6. Does the essay follow a logical organization? Why or why not?

Paragraph-level local revision questions

7. For each paragraph, answer the following questions:
   a. Is the paragraph important to the paper?
   b. Is the main point indicated clearly?
   c. Is the main point supported with relevant particulars?

Sentence-level local revision questions

8. Underline unclear sentences.

9. Cross out sentences that are unnecessary to the argument.

10. Indicate wordy or awkward sentences by placing a 'K' next to them.

11. Circle grammatical, spelling and punctuation errors.

Part B

Instructions

Accepting the perspective of the essay author, perform both a global and local revision of the essay. In other words, using the author's main arguments, write a 500–700 word essay that defends the reasonableness of believing in God.

29 Test preparation

For many students, taking tests can be an anxiety-producing event. In this chapter, we would like to offer some general advice about preparing for and taking tests. Though most of our advice is of a general nature, we finish the chapter with a few suggestions specific to taking tests in a philosophy course. We divide the test-taking process into four distinct stages: planning, studying, testing, evaluating.

Planning for a test is an essential first step towards success. Before you begin to study for a test, you should find out the answers to the following questions:

- How much of the final course grade is this test worth?
- What kind of test will it be?
- When and where is the test?
- How much time do I need to study for the test?
- When should I study?

Answers to the above questions should help you allocate your time well and help you choose appropriate study strategies. In cases where the test may have many parts and different types of questions, you should plan out a rough timeline for completion of the different sections. Hopefully, your instructor will provide you with enough information that you should be able to plan your studying sessions accordingly. However, if the instructor does not tell you what kind of test it will be, for example, then you should certainly ask her for more information.

The methods you use for studying should be mostly guided by the answers you discovered in the planning stage. For example, if you know that the test will be an essay test, as opposed to a multiple-choice, this should impact the nature of your studying. One of the most effective methods of studying for a test is to create and take your own tests on the material. If you know, for instance, that an upcoming test will include essay questions, a great way to study is to devise your own essay questions (based upon your class notes and the reading) and to then write out answers. When taking such practice tests, you should try to simulate the test environment as accurately as possible. So, for example, put yourself under time pressure and/or do not rely on your notes when taking a practice test (assuming these are the conditions under which you will be tested). If your test will require a good deal of recall of facts and terms, then the use of flash cards is a good idea (though combining this with a practice test would be even better). Organizing study sessions with peers is an effective way to study, especially if you quiz each other on the material, in either oral or written form. Reviewing your notes and re-reading the assigned material is another way to reinforce what you have learned, though such methods will not be as effective if done as an isolated (and more passive) activity. Whatever specific methods you use for studying, it is always a good idea to spread studying out over many sessions.

We offer the following basic pieces of advice, for when the time comes to take the test:

1. Read the instructions carefully.
2. Scan the entire test and devise a time management plan.
3. Ask questions if anything is unclear.
4. Follow specific advice, if any, of the instructor.
5. Use the entire time. If you finish early, take a mental break, and then go back and look over the test once more.

The suggestions above, we believe, are derived from common sense. However, we have noticed that a good number of students do not follow common sense when it comes to taking tests.

Finally, although it will not help you on the test just finished, it is important to review your test results to find out both your strengths and weaknesses. Also, if you are not satisfied with your performance on tests, then you ought to make changes to your methods of preparation and study. In other words, evaluate your study habits and, if they prove to be ineffective, find alternative methods of study for future tests.

The suggestions stated above are not specific to taking tests in a philosophy course. Given the wide variety of approaches to philosophy taken by instructors, it is difficult to offer specific advice that will always apply. Nevertheless, we believe the following suggestions would likely be helpful in many introductory courses.

- Familiarize yourself with philosophical terminology. During tests, most instructors will expect you to have a facility with philosophical terminology (see the exercises in Chapters 6–10 for assistance with some philosophical terms). Review your class notes and assigned readings to find the key terms of the course and spend a good deal of time studying them.
- Compare and contrast theories of philosophers you have studied. In many cases, instructors will take a historical approach to teaching philosophy and focus on the development of philosophical ideas through time. Since many philosophers write in response to other philosophers, understanding the similarities and differences of their ideas is very important for a thorough comprehension.
- Understand and be prepared to evaluate the arguments on a given philosophical topic. If your instructor spends a lot of time on dissecting arguments (as opposed to studying the history of philosophical ideas), it is likely that she takes a 'problems approach' to teaching philosophy. In that case, it is important for you to understand and evaluate the arguments themselves. Also, think about your own view on the topics and be prepared to defend them.

Exercise

Instructions

Before your next test, prepare for the test using as many of the test preparation suggestions as possible. After the test, write a short reflective essay on which methods seemed to have worked for you.

30 Putting it all together

Having introduced you to a variety of philosophical skills through-out this book, we think it appropriate to finish with a series of exercises requiring you to 'put it all together', that is, to employ and synthesize many of the skills learnt in previous chapters. For the exercises in this chapter, you will be asked to engage phil-osophically with the article 'Time and punishment' by the phi-losopher Christopher New and with two sample student essays written in response to a prompt. What this means is that while you are reading New's article, the prompt or the student essays, you should be asking yourself three questions: 'What skills am I using to understand the problem? What skills will I use to solve the problem? And, what skills will I use to analyze or evaluate my own conclusions?' You should find that many of the skills will appear useful in all of these contexts. Moreover, as you apply these skills in one context, they might, and usually will, affect the application of skills in a different context. In the end, this chapter should give you a full experience of what we have called 'doing philosophy'.

To achieve this experience in the following exercises, you will have to take one step back from many of the terms and methods of the previous chapters. We want to note this here to avoid any confusion. Our goal is that this exercise will allow you to produce a synthesis of the skills and not simply a brute regurgitation. This requires the following exercises to present the skills from previous chapters with some novelty. That is, you should not always expect an explicit question of the sort, 'How would you apply skill X here?'. Rather, we will ask you questions that require you to have a working knowledge of many of the skills mentioned to produce satisfactory answers. Moreover, we will also ask you questions that might only require you to perform more than one skill at a time to produce the best possible answer.

Given the goals of this chapter, we have provided our own answers to all of the questions in the following exercises. We think the best strategy for using this resource would be to refer to these answers only after you have done the best you can to answer all the questions on your own. Once you have done this, we suggest that you compare your answers with ours. Another strategy would be to compare answers as you complete the exercises. In this way, you will also begin to see how the use of these skills in particular contexts relate to the context of the whole process of doing philosophy.

By the end, you should have a clearer understanding of how to apply these skills 'in the wild' of your course work in a philosophy class. We are hopeful that you will, as well, have a clearer understanding of how to use the skills more generally to improve your work in other academic pursuits and improve your ability to think critically in a wide variety of contexts.

Exercise

Part A

Instructions
Read the following article titled 'Time and punishment' by the philosopher Christopher New. After reading each paragraph, answer the questions (if any) on the right of the paragraph.

Article: 'Time and punishment'[1]

I

We have a strong intuition that it is wrong to punish someone for a crime he has not committed, and it is, indeed, often considered a criterion of any adequate theory of punishment that the theory disallow such punishments. Punishing someone for a crime he has not committed is easily identified

1. Do you share the intuition that it would always be wrong to punish someone for a crime not yet committed? Why or why not?

with punishing the innocent, and that is no doubt partly why we do not usually bother to question our intuition – how could we be justified in punishing the innocent? Nevertheless, I think this identification is misleading, and I am going to describe an example which seems to undermine the intuition. If this example is valid, it suggests that there may be room in our moral thought for the notion of prepunishment, and that it may be only epistemic, rather than moral, constraints that prevent us from practising it. By 'prepunishment' I mean punishment for an offence before the offence is committed; I shall use 'postpunishment' to mean punishment after the offence has been committed. This leaves open the possibility of 'syncpunishment' – a punishment while the offence is being committed. I shall not discuss syncpunishment explicitly, but I assume that whatever case can be made for prepunishment can be made *mutatis mutandis* for sync-punishment also.

II

My example is this. Ben, a philosophical, Alaskan traffic policeman, and Algy, an eccentric, casuistical speedster, both know that Algy now intends, will continue to intend, and will eventually carry out his intention to exceed the speed limit on a remote, unpatrolled, but radar-surveyed stretch of Wilderness One at 10.31 tomorrow morning. They know this by virtue of (a) Algy's introspective awareness of his own intentions;

2. Which of the following statements best paraphrases the author's main thesis?
 (a) We might find moral room for the concept of prepunishment.
 (b) Prepunishment might be morally acceptable despite our intuition against it.
 (c) There may be cases in which punishing the innocent is not morally problematic.

3. The author claims that both Ben and Algy 'know' that Algy is going to commit the crime. Evaluate this claim. Would you say that Ben and Algy 'know' that Algy is going to commit the crime?

(b) Ben's and Algy's non-introspective awareness of Algy's intentions, character, abilities and resources (we may suppose this includes complex neurophysiological information); (c) Ben's and Algy's awareness of the condition of Wilderness One, Algy's car and the inability of Alaska's finest to trace Algy or reach the distant scene of the offence until several hours after the misdemeanour has been committed. Algy, whilst remaining out of reach, radios Ben with the following offer: If Ben issues the fixed penalty summons for this violation before it occurs, he will pay the fine before he commits the offence. But if Ben does not issue the summons until after the offence, Algy will skip the country and avoid paying the fine. Algy and Ben both know Algy is speaking the truth here, by the same means that they know he is going to commit the offence. After some reflection, Ben decides to issue the summons now, writing in tomorrow's date as the date of the violation. He delivers the ticket to Algy's nearby address, whereupon Algy's wife hands over Algy's cheque for the fine, which he has left with her in a sealed envelope. The cheque is cashed immediately, and at 10.31 the next day Algy exceeds the speed limit on Wilderness One exactly as described in his fixed penalty summons.

What objections (apart from those arising from existing legislation) can we raise against this case of prepunishment? One might be that what I have described is not a case of prepunishment at all, but,

4. To which branch of philosophy does the third question belong?

5. Do you think the example shows what the author intended to show? Explain.

6. Evaluate the following argument for validity and soundness.
Premise: The example of Ben and Algy is really an example of postpunishment and not prepunishment.
Conclusion: Thus, the example does not support New's thesis that prepunishment may be morally acceptable.

rather, of postpunishment – postpunishment of a different offence. Algy is being punished for the offence of *planning* to exceed the speed limit, it might be held, and the punishment is imposed *after* that offence is committed. But that is not so; my example specifies that Algy's offence is that of *speeding at 10.31 tomorrow,* not of *planning today to speed at 10.31 tomorrow.* If the latter offence existed, it would perhaps be possible both to postpunish Algy for planning to exceed the speed limit and to prepunish him for actually exceeding it. But there is no question that what Algy is punished for in my example is exceeding the speed limit tomorrow, not planning today to exceed it tomorrow.

Some would perhaps object that in the case I have described, Ben and Algy do not have knowledge but only rational belief about Algy's future actions. This expresses a scepticism many do not share, but I will not discuss it here. For even if we were to concede that Ben's and Algy's state is not knowledge, but only rational belief, Ben would still apparently be justified, as I shall argue in Section III, in accepting Algy's prepunishment offer. For Ben's belief is surely based on evidence which puts it beyond reasonable doubt that Algy will commit the offence, and proof beyond reasonable doubt is all we ever require when we find someone guilty and punish him. So though I shall continue to speak of *knowledge* here, the sceptic may mentally substitute *rational belief* without affecting the main point I am

7. In this paragraph, New claims it does not matter whether Ben and Algy really 'know' Algy will speed. Instead, it only matters that Ben has no reasonable doubt in believing that Algy will speed. Given the scenario described, is it beyond reasonable doubt that Algy will speed? Explain.

making – that prepunishment appears to be sometimes a justifiable procedure.

Those who accept that Ben's and Algy's state would indeed be knowledge may object that nevertheless it is a state that never in fact occurs. This, however, is irrelevant. I do not claim that anyone will ever have such knowledge, only that it is coherent to suppose that someone might. Some will perhaps contest this, holding that my example is in some way incoherent. If that were so, of course, it could be rejected. But I know of no argument which proves that there could never be such knowledge about a person's future actions. So I think this objection is at best non-proven. We are provisionally justified, therefore, in holding that the example is coherent.

These objections are epistemic. Let us consider now whether either of the main theories of punishment provide moral grounds for rejecting our example. Retributivists hold that punishment is justified, not by any deterrent effect it may have, but by the fact that the offender in some way *deserves* to suffer for his offence. But there is nothing in this view, thus stated, which prescribes that he should suffer *after* rather than *before* the offence. Nevertheless, retributivists may maintain, we all hold, or should hold, the principle that it is wrong to punish an innocent person; and punishing Algy before he commits his offence infringes that principle, since it is punishing him while he is innocent. But Ben may reply that we should distinguish between two forms of this principle.

8. Do you think the author commits an *appeal to ignorance* fallacy here?

9. Find one normative claim and one descriptive claim made by either the retributivist or the author in this paragraph.

The first form is that it is wrong to punish someone for an offence he *never commits*, the second that it is wrong to punish someone for an offence which all involved know he *intends to and will commit* after his punishment. Ben may contend that it is the first form of the principle we should uphold, not the second; for the second is not in a morally significant way punishing the innocent at all. Indeed, in our example, if we uphold the second form, we knowingly allow Algy to commit an offence and get off scot-free; which retributivists ought to find morally repugnant.

10. If you had to pick one sentence that captures the main point of this paragraph, which sentence would it be?

An analogy comes to mind here, though it is not exact in every way. We must pay for goods we obtain from others, Ben may point out; and if we don't pay after delivery, we must pay before. Why shouldn't it be the same with punishment? We must pay for our offences, the retributivist affirms. Very well, then; and if we don't pay after committing them, we must pay before. All that is required is that everyone involved should know the punished person deserves the penalty; and in this case surely that condition is satisfied. To those who insist that a person does not *become* guilty, and so deserve the penalty, until he actually commits an offence, Ben may reply either that this is mere prejudice, attaching improper moral significance to an insignificant temporal fact, or that the plausibility of their position depends on the assumption that we do not *know* an offence will be committed until it actually has been committed (in which case we

11. The author uses an analogy to support his view. Paraphrase the analogy in 3–4 sentences and then determine whether the analogy works.

12. What does *ex hypothesi* mean?

never know it *will* be committed) – an assumption which is *ex hypothesi* not true in this case. If it is known to all involved in a commercial transaction that the purchaser will take the goods, the vendor has no particular reason to prefer postpayment to prepayment, Ben may point out. Equally, if it is known to all involved that Algy intends, will continue to intend, and will eventually carry out his intention to commit the speeding offence, we should have no reason to prefer postpunishment to prepunishment. And in this case we would have a reason not to prefer it: postpunishment is impossible. What is there in retributivist theory that shows Ben is mistaken?

Some may object that we are punishing Algy because he is *going* to become guilty rather than because he *has become* so – but why is this an *objection*? If all involved knew both that there would be a typhoon tomorrow and that the responsible forecaster now intended, would continue to intend, and would eventually carry out his intention not to issue a typhoon warning in due time, we wouldn't think twice about demoting him now rather than waiting until the due time was upon us (or past) – particularly if we also knew we couldn't demote him afterwards. Why, Ben may demand, should we think twice about prepunishing Algy, then? It is not easy to see what a retributivist can reply.

At first sight it may seem that deterrence theorists will be able to reject our example quite easily. They may be tempted to say it is wrong to prepunish

> 13. The author responds to another possible objection with a different analogy. Is Algy relevantly similar to the forecaster? Explain.

> 14. What is a 'deterrence theorist'?

Algy because *ex hypothesi* doing so won't deter him from committing the future crime for which he is now punished. But Ben has a ready answer here. The same is true of postpunishment, he can observe, which manifestly does not deter the offender from committing the offence for which he is punished. And in pre- as much as in postpunishment the penalty imposed may deter potential offenders, as also the actual offender, from committing *other* offences in the future. If we all assume that this is so in Algy's case, the deterrence theorist is after all in no better state than the retributivist to reject our example. Of course, if we modified it, by supposing, say, that the world was going to end immediately after Algy's misdemeanour, deterrence theorists would have a reason unavailable to retributivists for rejecting prepunishment. For then *ex hypothesi* no deterrent effect whatsoever would be obtainable from prepunishment. But the unmodified example does not allow the deterrence theorist this way out.

Reflecting on Ben's commercial analogy, someone might object that prepunishment appears to involve the surely wrong idea that after the offender has been punished he has a *right* to commit his offence, just as, after a person has prepaid for his goods, he has a right to collect them. But this is to be misled by the analogy, which, as I said earlier, is not exact. The purchaser does, indeed, have a right to his goods, because that is part of the implicit or explicit contract he has made with the vendor. But no such

15. How would New evaluate the following argument?
Premise 1: The only morally legitimate reason to punish criminals is to deter them from committing future crimes.
Premise 2: Punishing someone for a crime not yet committed will not deter them from committing the crime.
Conclusion: There is no morally legitimate reason for prepunishment.

16. The author entertains another possible argument against his view. Paraphrase the argument and put it into standard form.

17. What is the least compelling claim the author makes in this paragraph?

contract exists between the offender and the authorities. It is definitive of an offence that the perpetrator has no right to commit it. What our example tells us is that Algy will commit the offence; from this we can infer that no-one will prevent him from committing it. But we cannot infer from that, or from the fact that he has already been punished, that he has a *right to commit it.*

This reply may give rise to another objection. If nothing we do will prevent him from committing his offence, it may be said, then Algy is not a fit subject for punishment of any kind, pre- or post-; he must be an uninfluenceable psychopath. But this objection, too, is mistaken. It may be true that a person who *cannot* be deterred or dissuaded by any means whatsoever from committing an offence is not a proper subject for punishment. But we have no reason to suppose that Algy is such a person. All we know is that he *will not in fact* be deterred or dissuaded, not that he cannot be. There may be any number of reasons why he is not prevented from speeding on Wilderness One, and we are entitled to assume in our example that Algy is like most of us – someone who wants to do something, is able to do it, and is not prevented; he is not an uninfluenceable psychopath, but as proper a subject for punishment as anyone ever is.

III

We have been considering a particular case in which prepunishment appears to be justified; are there limits to how

18. The author argues the death penalty puts a limit on prepunishment. Paraphrase the argument and put it into standard form.

far we can go? One limit is clearly suggested by the death penalty. If Algy's crime on Wilderness One were not speeding, but the hatchet murder of a lone hiker, for instance, and if murder attracted the death penalty, it would not be possible both to know that he would commit this murder and to impose the death penalty by way of prepunishment, since his execution would prevent the commission of the offence for which he was to be executed. At first sight this might lead us to suppose that foreknowledge could paradoxically *prevent* us from imposing the death penalty. But, of course, this is not so. If we know he is going to commit this murder, it follows that we will not execute him first; but our failure to do so will be due to Algy's diabolically elusive cunning, our own constabulary incompetence, judicial corruption or some other cause. What it cannot be due to is our knowledge that he is going to commit this murder. Our knowledge that he will do so *entails* that we fail to execute him beforehand; it does not *cause* us so to fail.

Another limit might be on the period within which we would be prepared to countenance prepunishment, just as we may think there is a limit on the period within which we are willing to countenance postpunishment. An offender might be very old or very young, or the time between his punishment and his offence might be very long, or he might be very ill; and these considerations might make us reluctant to prepunish at a certain time, just as they may make us

19. Paraphrase the main claim of this paragraph in one sentence.

reluctant to postpunish. In this respect pre- and postpunishment seem identical.

There is one way in which we should be willing to go further than our original example allows. (In doing so, we will satisfy the sceptics who doubt whether Ben and Algy really *know* what Algy is going to do.) We have been postulating that all involved should *know* that the offence was intended and would be committed. But isn't this requirement too stringent? It is not, after all, a requirement of postpunishment, where what we demand is not *knowledge* that the accused committed the offence, but proof *beyond reasonable doubt*. Suppose we similarly relaxed the requirement for prepunishment, demanding only that it was beyond reasonable doubt that the accused would commit a certain crime. Then it might turn out, admittedly, as it sometimes does with postpunishment, that we had punished a person unjustly, though in good faith; moreover, it might not be possible to redress the injustice, since he might have died in the interval between the infliction of his punishment and the establishment of his innocence. But this is a hazard of postpunishment also; so if we accept the risk in one case, it would seem inconsistent not to accept it in the other.

IV

Prepunishment is a strange notion, admittedly, then, but not one which seems to be clearly excluded by epistemic or logical considerations, or by

20. Is the conclusion effective? Why or why not?

either of the main theories of punishment. We may be reminded here of backward causation, an idea which at first seems absurd, but which neither logical considerations nor causal theories may seem immediately to exclude. It seems possible in both cases to make these strange notions appear intelligible. In the case of punishment, of course, we cannot now satisfy, and may never be able to satisfy, the epistemic condition for practising prepunishment. But the question is: is it only our lack of foreknowledge that prevents us, or is there some deeper moral objection to it? My suggestion is that there is no deeper moral objection.

Part B

Instructions

Read the following instructor prompt and the student essay written in response to it. As you read the essay, answer the questions (if any) in the side pagination to the right of the paragraph.

Instructor prompt

Prepunishment is the practice of punishing a person before a crime has been committed. In the article 'Time and Punishment', Christopher New argues that our beliefs about why we should or should not practice prepunishment are mistaken. Evaluate New's arguments and then formulate a response that supports his central claim or shows where he is mistaken.

Essay 1: 'How can we know the future?'

How can we know what a person will do tomorrow? The essential problem with Christopher New's argument for 'prepunishment' in the article 'Time and punishment' is that we can never know what a person might do in the future. In the Steven Spielberg movie *Minority Report* the main character, John Anderton, faces just such a problem of being pre-punished for a crime he has yet to commit. The movie's plot resolves this problem by demonstrating that Anderton could still choose a different path. This is just one way in which New's argument could be undermined. There are a number of ways that the future might change from what we expect it to be. Once we look at these, we can see that New's argument is nothing more than a flight of fancy.

What if Algy blows a tire on Wilderness One? New claims that both Algy and Ben have a lot of information that will guarantee that Algy will commit the crime of speeding. He claims that they know things like 'the conditions of Wilderness One, Algy's car' (New, 35) and other facts about the conditions of the event. The problem with this stipulation is that these are just assumptions that could have no basis in facts. There is no way to be certain that Algy won't blow a tire, swerve to miss a deer, or encounter a bridge that is out. All of these things are plausible or likely events that could occur to prevent Algy from committing the crime. This type of uncertainty is

> 1. What is the author's thesis? On the basis of that thesis, does it seem to you that the author focuses on the relevant philosophical issues?

> 2. What do you think of the tone and structure of the student essay thus far? Is it clear, objective and effective at laying out the argument?

easy to prove. How many times have you been surprised by events? Human life is full of all kinds of surprises – cheating spouses, blown radiators, tsunamis – why should we believe that Algy and Ben are any different from us? It doesn't matter how well you know conditions, they always change and always will. Because this is true, there is no reason Ben could know Algy would speed. Algy can't even know he will speed, unless he has a crystal ball that can show him the future.

What if Algy is lying? New also claims, fantastically I might add, that Ben knows 'Algy's intentions' (New, 35). But if Algy is such a bad guy, why should we believe that he isn't trying to trick Ben to get some sort of legal revenge on his nemesis. This just goes to my original point that we can't ever know the sorts of things New claims to know about Algy. People lie all the time, so these so-called facts are far from sure. The possibility that someone could be deceiving you should cause us to doubt all kinds of claims that people make. Algy is apparently the exact sort of person we should be suspicious of. New doesn't seem to see that creating a guy like Algy, who would call to make a deal with Ben about committing a crime, contradicts the point he's trying to make. How can we trust Algy? We can't, and because we can't trust him New's whole argument rests on a contradiction.

We can't trust Algy, but can we even trust Ben, or ourselves? Here is where Jon Anderton comes back into the picture. Men always have a choice; they

3. At the end of this paragraph, the student claims there is a 'contradiction' in New's argument. Explain and evaluate this claim.

4. What do you think of the author's integration of the movie *Minority Report* into her argument? Is it effective? Why or why not?

can always choose to do something different. Anderton was convicted of the pre-murder of Leo Crow. He then struggles to escape and prove his innocence. Throughout the movie we see many examples of the two problems I pointed to above. First, there are lots of changes to expected events. Many times when you think that Anderton is captured or that some event is going to end his life, he escapes or something happens that gets him off the hook. Second, the entire plot is driven by the lies of Anderton's boss, Lamar Burgess. The pre-cogs, the hive mind that reveals the future in the movie, are defeated by his deception. These alone should be enough to show that we cannot know the future. However, the most troubling event for New's argument is Anderton's choice not to kill Crow. Even with all the lies, deception and blown tires, Anderton still finds himself holding a gun on Leo Crow. But, instead of killing him he chooses not to. This is the biggest hole in New's argument. Even if we can know there are no liars around, even if the event in question is simple and easy to forecast, human beings still have a choice.

Don't we have a choice to do something different? This is the biggest problem with New's argument. Algy, you, and I could always choose to do something different. Because of this ability to choose, there could never be a good argument for his 'prepunishment'. We would quite literally be punishing Algy or any other person for something that they have not done, and could still yet not do.

Because we still have a choice, we can always choose differently. This is why 'postpunishment' is ok. We can always choose, but we can never go back in time and change our choices. Our freedom only goes one way.

Thomas New's argument in 'Time and punishment' is completely fantastical. We can simply never know what might happen, who is lying, and what we might choose to do. Algy can blow a tire, Alaska could suffer an earthquake, or the Wilderness One highway could be closed tomorrow. In that case we have punished an innocent man. Why should we trust Algy, or anyone else? People lie all the time and Algy could be lying now. If he had lied we wouldn't have punished an innocent man, but we would have punished him for the wrong reason. Finally, we always have a choice to do differently. What would we do if Algy was just coming up to the speed limit of Wilderness One and suddenly felt a pang of guilt and reformed his ways? In that case we would have punished an innocent man for making the exact right choice we wanted him to make. We cannot ever know until after a choice is made and the event occurs if men are guilty or not. Punishing ahead of time is punishing innocent people.

5. By the end of Essay 1 do you think you have a good impression of the author's main argument? Did the author's conclusion reinforce this impression?

Part C

Instructions

Read the following student essay written in response to the prompt in Part B of this exercise. As you read the essay, answer the questions (if any) in the side pagination to the right of the paragraph.

Essay 2 : 'A critique of New's view of punishment'

In 'Time and punishment', Christopher New argues that there is nothing morally wrong with the idea of 'prepunishment', which is punishing someone for a crime before he has committed it. According to New, the only plausible objection to prepunishment is that we cannot know what will happen in the future. This objection, New says, is merely an epistemic one regarding what we can know and not a moral one about what is right or wrong. As New says, 'there may be room in our moral thought for the notion of pre-punishment, and that it may be only epistemic, rather than moral, constraints that prevent us from practising it'.[2] In other words, New asserts that if we could know what will happen in the future, then we should have no moral objection to 'prepunishment.' In this paper I will argue that New is mistaken and that 'prepunishment' is morally wrong. 'Prepunishment' is wrong because it punishes the innocent despite New's claim to the contrary. My argument will summarize New's position, examine some of the assumptions he makes, and then argue for the correct view of 'punishment', one that punishes the guilty while respecting human rights.

New's argument relies on a thought experiment that involves Algy, a man intent on speeding, but who is willing to pay a fine before he actually speeds. In this scenario, Algy notifies Ben, a policeman, that he will speed tomorrow. In this counterfactual scenario, both Algy

> 1. What is the author's thesis? On the basis of that thesis, do you think the author focuses on the relevant philosophical issues?

and Ben know that Algy will speed 'by virtue of (a) Algy's introspective awareness of his own intentions; (b) Ben's and Algy's non-introspective awareness of Algy's intentions, character, abilities and resources (we may suppose this includes complex neurophysiological information); (c) Ben's and Algy's awareness of the condition of Wilderness One, Algy's car, and the inability of Alaska's finest to trace Algy or reach the distant scene of the offence until several hours after the misdemeanour has been committed.'[3] Since Ben and Algy 'know' that Algy will speed, New contends, there is nothing morally wrong with Ben giving Algy a speeding ticket before Algy speeds.

New cites and responds to the obvious objection that Ben does not really 'know' that Algy will speed. His answer is that knowledge of a crime, whether before or after a crime is committed, does not require certainty, rather only requires knowing beyond a reasonable doubt. And 'Ben's belief is surely based on evidence which puts it beyond reasonable doubt that Algy will commit the offence', New says, 'and proof beyond reasonable doubt is all we ever require when we find someone guilty and punish him'.[4] Since the standard of knowing beyond a reasonable doubt applies in both pre- and postpunishment, there is no moral difference between them. In other words, New argues, we can know beyond a reasonable doubt that Algy will speed, and it is, therefore, right to punish him before he does so.

Appealing to our strong intuition in favour of justice, New further claims that the counterfactual shows the choice is really between prepunishment and no punishment at all. Either Algy pays the fine up front and speeds, or he speeds, doesn't get caught, and thus avoids punishment. If we don't prepunish Algy, New claims, then he is allowed to commit two transgressions without any form of punishment at all: intending to break the law and then actually breaking it. Further, New claims that prepunishment actually respects Algy by taking his intentions seriously. Additionally, justice is served by not allowing a crime to go unpunished.

New raises and responds to the objection that prepunishment could lead to wrongly punishing the innocent. He responds by recalling that we sometimes punish the innocent in the normal case of postpunishment and, in some cases, we don't believe that the jury was morally wrong to do so. When we find them guilty, punish them and later find that their conviction was based on error, we do not hold the jury and prosecutors liable for a moral failing (as long as the error was unintentional). Instead, we think that they made a mistake. New argues that we are willing to allow this mistake in postpunishment, so why not with prepunishment? Again, he claims the objection is epistemic, not moral. With the standard for postpunishment established as knowing beyond a reasonable doubt, does having the knowledge that Algy will speed meet this criterion? According

2. By the end of this paragraph, the author will finish summarizing New's article. Did the author write a good description of New's argument?

to New, it does, and this knowledge is adequate for prepunishing Algy.

Although New sees no moral difference between pre- and postpunishment, there is an important difference that he does not acknowledge, namely, the ability of the supposed criminal to change his mind. While this is not an issue for postpunishment, since you cannot decide to 'undo' something you have done, it does seem to be an issue for prepunishment. New's argument rests on at least one unsupported claim. His argument implies (without argument) the truth of determinism, which holds that humans are determined by previous events to commit the actions we do. New is essentially claiming that Algy is determined to commit the crime in a way that makes it similar to an act already committed in the past. If determinism is true, then moral innocence has little value because people are not responsible for their actions. If I am forced to do X, in other words, then I am not free to do otherwise, thus I should not be held accountable for doing X. Here is how I see it playing out in New's thought experiment: in this scenario, Algy seems determined to speed, and if hard determinism is true, he is not guilty of a crime. Of course if hard determinism is true, no one is responsible (and, therefore not guilty or innocent) of anything. However, this view deeply violates our intuitions about free will. Morality is not real in such a world, but morality seems to be one of the most important elements of human experience.

Prepunishment, in my opinion, does not respect the choice of individuals.

> 3. Paraphrase and evaluate the author's objection, in the paragraph, to New's argument.

To treat Algy morally is to treat him as someone capable of choosing not to speed, so prepunishment fails to treat Algy morally because it does not respect his right to choose. Therefore, using prepunishment to fight crime would not respect the choice of individuals.

Another problem with New's argument is his reliance on a faulty analogy when he compares prepunishment to prepayment for goods from a vendor. New concludes that to claim since we have no reason to prefer postpayment to prepayment for goods, there is no moral significant difference between pre- and postpunishment. However, this analogy fails because New compares two unlike analogs: a legal purchase of goods is not morally similar to a criminal act to warrant comparison; therefore, any conclusions based on this analogy are unfounded. The natural rules and intuitions that we have about legal transactions are not equivalent to the ones we have regarding illegal ones, so conclusions that follow from such an argument rest on faulty reasoning.

> 4. Choose the most important claim in this paragraph and evaluate it.

Let's look at the conclusion that New sees this analogy entailing: the belief that a person only 'become[s] guilty' after committing the crime gives 'improper moral significance to an insignificant temporal fact',[5] namely that the event has not happened yet. This view of innocence seems to violate our deepest beliefs about this primary moral concept. This understanding of innocence renders this moral concept merely instrumental to justice instead of acknowledging the intrinsic moral value of innocence. In other words, innocence is not merely a tool we ought to use in determining whether to punish a person for a crime or not; rather innocence is an intrinsically valuable moral category. In New's view, innocence serves the purpose of justice, but this view reverses the proper moral order. Rather, justice, a concept that only has meaning in terms of its service to the innocent, should serve the innocent. Justice is not some independent concept that requires our service. Consider the U.S. legal system; it appears to reflect this bias toward protecting the innocent even if it means allowing some guilty defendants to go free.

Although New presents some interesting analysis of the role of epistemology in the concept of punishment in his thought experiment, he fails to account for the most important aspects: free will and innocence. I have shown how he fails on both accounts; first, holding Algy responsible for a future crime is viewing him as a person incapable of doing otherwise instead of respecting his ability to choose, making him (and everyone else for that matter) unworthy of blame or praise. Second, prepunishing Algy fails to show respect for the primary moral concept of innocence. Knowing that our epistemology is such that we will rarely (if ever) have absolute certainty about a defendant's guilt or innocence, we find that the possibility of allowing some who are guilty to go free is morally preferable to allowing the conviction of some innocent. Certainly pointing to our intuitions

5. Is this an effective conclusion?

is not free from criticism, for our intuitions could be wrong, but for now, that's
the most we can hope for. Until the matter of determinism is resolved, we cannot
know for sure whether we have free will
at all. And finally of course, the fact that
our legal system reflects our moral intuitions merely means that if our intuitions
are wrong, so is our legal system.

Part D

Instructions

Reread the previous student essays and then answer the questions
that follow.

1. Put the main argument of Essay 1 into standard form.
2. Put the main argument of Essay 2 into standard form.
3. Which student essay better demonstrates an understanding
    of the role of New's counterfactual scenario and its role in
    his argument?
4. Which student essay better focuses on the correct philo-
    sophical issue at stake in New's argument? Explain your
    answer.
5. Which student essay avoids common informal fallacies?
6. The essay authors present a different understanding of
    New's argument. How does this difference affect their
    respective evaluations of his argument?
7. Which student essay does a better job using quotations?
    Explain your answer.
8. Which student essay has a better introduction and conclu-
    sion? Explain your answer.
9. Which student essay is clearer and easier to understand?
    Explain your answer.
10. Imagine that you are the instructor grading these papers.
    Which is a better example of doing philosophy in response
    to the prompt?

Answers to selected exercises

Chapter 1

Part A
1. NP
5. NP
9. P

Part B

1. Is it right for basketball players to cheat? Is gambling something that the law should ever recognize as acceptable? Is it the government's role to prevent cheating?

Chapter 2

Part A
The following sample answers used chapter 16 from Blocker, H. G. and Petrick, J. and Stewart, D. (2010), *The Fundamentals of Philosophy*. Boston: Prentice Hall.

1. The title of the chapter is 'The Quest for Certainty' and it is a chapter in Part 4 (called 'How Do We Know? Epistemology') of a secondary source philosophy textbook.
2. I have learned that epistemology is the study of knowledge, so I suspect that this chapter will have something to do with the question 'How we know?' Since the specific title is 'The Quest for Certainty', the chapter will probably have to do with trying to find out how we know something for certain.

3. The subtitles in this chapter and what they reveal are:

   a. *Search for a Method.* This might be about the search for a method to achieve 'certainty' in knowledge (since the chapter title is 'Quest for Certainty').

   b. *Grounds for Doubt.* This might be about reasons why people doubt things.

   c. *Cogito Ergo Sum.* I have no idea what this means, so I should probably find out.

   d. *The Role of the Senses.* This might be about how the senses help us achieve certainty in knowledge.

4. There are no boldfaced words or phrases. There are four long highlighted passages. The highlighted passages and what they reveal are:

   a. *Montaigne on Scepticism.* I have not heard of Montaigne, but I suspect he is sceptical of achieving certainty.

   b. *Rene Descartes: First Meditation Concerning Things That Can Be Doubted.* It looks as though this passage is written by someone named Descartes and he is writing about knowledge that is doubtful.

   c. *Second Meditation on the Nature of the Human Mind and That It Is More Easily Known Than the Body.* It seems that Descartes also believes that the mind is more easily known than the body, though this seems strange since I know more about the human body than minds.

   d. *The Wax Example.* I have no idea what this example is about.

Part B

One theory of truth is the *pragmatic* theory. Pragmatism, a native American philosophical school which began with the work of Charles Sanders Peirce in the nineteenth century, emphasizes the close relationship between thinking and acting. Indeed, thinking is viewed by the pragmatists as problem-solving activity. Ideas are plans of action; the meaning of ideas or terms is reducible to their concrete, practical implications. On the subject of truth, pragmatists tell us that a statement is true if, when we act upon it, we actually encounter the consequences which the statement implies, anticipates, or predicts. Every meaningful statement, they argue, can be translated into a set of consequences which is supposed to follow if specific operations are performed. So perform the operations, and observe whether the consequences ensue. If so, the statement is true; if not, it is false. [For instance, let us suppose that your doctor diagnoses an ailment of yours as an allergy to chlorine, which you encounter frequently since swimming is one of your hobbies. Is his or her diagnosis, formulated in the statement, 'You are allergic to chlorine', true or false? This statement implies that you should stop swimming and exposing yourself to chlorine for a time, then the ailment will disappear. If you do the former, and the latter ensues, a pragmatist would say that the doctor's statement is true; if the ailment continues, however, the diagnosis would be false.]

> Criticism: My professor says pragmatists believe truth is what is 'useful'. Seems like a different view.
>
> ? Confusing
>
> Summary: Pragmatists say truth is confirmed by consequences.

Chapter 3

No answers

Chapter 4

No answers

Chapter 5

1. This is primarily a question of political philosophy because answering this question requires us to make claims about the obligations and duties of citizens to one's own government. I can also classify it as an ethical question because it concerns claims about what is right or wrong.

4. This is primarily a metaphysical question because it is making a fundamental claim about the nature of reality, namely, that mental reality is the same as physical reality.

10. This is an epistemological question about the conditions of knowledge.

12. This is primarily a question concerning ethics since it is about the morality of something.

Chapter 6

1. b
5. a
9. b

Chapter 7

1. a
5. a
10. b

Chapter 8

1. b
5. b
9. b

Chapter 9

1. b
5. b
9. a

Chapter 10

1. b
5. b
9. c

Chapter 11

1. b. The passage is asking whether a person who has no objections to being in a locked room is 'free'. This raises the question

about the nature of voluntary actions. The passage does not really suggest anything about finding a middle ground between free and involuntary actions, as in answer a. Also, while the passage says something about happiness, it is not concerned with figuring out if voluntary action is 'always' related to choice.

2. I think a person is not free to leave the room, thus that person is not acting voluntarily. To say that a person is 'free', I believe, means that the person has real options to choose from. If a man is locked in a room, he does not have the real option of leaving, hence staying in the room is not voluntary.

3. Metaphysics. Metaphysics is the branch of philosophy that raises fundamental questions about the nature of reality and human existence. Specifically, Locke's thought experiment considers the nature of human freedom. There is no mention of religion or God, so it is not d. It also does not raise any questions about right and wrong actions, so it is not c. It does ask a question about something we might know, but it does not specifically ask questions about knowledge itself. Thus, it is not a.

Chapter 12

Part A
1. Claim (normative)
4. Not a claim.

Part B
1. Descriptive
5. Normative

Part C
1. *A posteriori*
5. *A priori*

Chapter 13

Part A
1. Neither
5. Inconsistent

Part B
1. The author's view of death is clearly expressed, except for the claim that death might be 'a change from here to another place'.

This is not clear because it does not say what kind of 'change' nor does it provide any information about 'another place'.

2. The author claims that if death were a dreamless sleep, it would be pleasant. It is not obvious to me whether this is compatible with established facts. Is it even possible to feel pleasure while one is sleeping? Also, could death be some third option?

3. The author seems to be inconsistent when he talks about what we can know about death. At first, he says 'no one knows whether death may be the greatest of blessings', but then he claims that he knows that death is one of two things, both of which are good.

Chapter 14

Part A

1. Premise. A discipline is worthless if it does not provide definitive answers.

5. Premise. Moral travesties must be stopped.

Part B

1. Premise: Only those soldiers with the necessary strength to perform in combat should be allowed to join combat units (implied premise).

   Premise: Women (for the most part) do not have the necessary strength to perform in combat.

   Conclusion: Women should continue to be barred from combat units.

Chapter 15

1. Argument, deductive.
5. No argument.
9. Argument, deductive.

Chapter 16

Part A
1. Valid
5. Valid

Part B
6. Sound
10. Unsound

Part C
11. Weak
15. Strong

Part D
16. Cogent
20. Not cogent

Chapter 17

No Answers

Chapter 18

Part A
1. *Ad populum*
5. *Ad hominem*
9. *Ad ignorantium*

Chapter 19

1. ~~Can you believe that there are people who call themselves Americans who think ownership of firearms is wrong? What kind of Americans do they think they are?~~ [The second amendment to the United States *Constitution* establishes the right to bear arms.] [The *Constitution*, ~~we should remember~~, is not only a legal document, but a moral one]. *So it is not wrong for U. S. citizens to own a gun for personal use.* ~~We should send everyone who favors gun control to Mexico where they will wish they owned a gun~~.

Premise 1: The second amendment to the United States *Constitution* establishes the right to bear arms.

Premise 2: The *Constitution* is not only a legal document, but a moral one.

Conclusion: It is not wrong for U. S. citizens to own a gun for personal use.

5. ~~When travelling to other countries, one of the aspects of those~~ ~~foreign lands you might notice is the fact that~~ [societies seem to have different moral standards.] ~~In some countries, a man may~~ ~~have more than one wife. Others have legalized prostitution~~ ~~or marijuana use. Some even allow for euthanizing the old. In~~ ~~our country, permitting these behaviours seems unthinkable to~~ ~~most. How could it be that there are so many moral principles~~ ~~that cultures disagree upon? The most reasonable explanation~~ ~~seems to be that there are no universal moral concepts or prin-~~ ~~ciples that apply to every culture.~~ *Therefore, moral absolutism is wrong and moral relativism is true.*

Premise: Different societies have different moral standards
Conclusion: Moral absolutism is wrong and moral relativism is true.

Chapter 20

No answers

Chapter 21

Part B
1. Yes. It is problematic, significant and interesting.
5. No. It seems obvious to me that scientific evidence should not be ignored, thus this question does not seem very problematic, though the general topic of truth and knowledge is both significant and interesting.
9. No. It is not problematic, but a clear fact that Hitler was a war criminal.

Chapter 22

No answers

Chapter 23

1. Summary 1
5. Summary 1

Chapter 24

1. Number 3 best paraphrases the passage. Number 1 is too close to the original wording of the passage. Number 2 is not as accurate as number 3.

5. Number 3 most accurately describes the question raised by the passage.

Chapter 25

1. Student evaluation 2 does the best job of exposing false, unsupported and questionable claims because it clearly shows some of the problems with J. Gay-William's argument. Student evaluation 1 might be slightly better than evaluation 3 because the latter does not really explain or state clearly the objections. What, for example, is a 'fallacy of composition'? The student does not explain this.

Chapter 26

Part A

1. The author of the passage is making an argument for a woman's right to an abortion by way of an analogy. If you were stuck in a house with a rapidly growing child, the author claims, you would have the right to kill this child when its continued growth threatens your own life. 'However innocent the child may be', the author says, 'you do not have to wait passively while it crushes you to death'. Similarly, a woman has a right to an abortion if the growing fetus threatens the mother's life.

Part B

1. This is not a good use of a quotation, though it is formatted correctly, since the phrase 'accomplished a lot' is not very meaningful to the main idea of the passage.

Chapter 27

No Answers

Chapter 28

No answers

Chapter 29

No answers

Chapter 30

Part A

1. I share this intuition because a person should be punished only if guilty of a crime. A person, however, cannot be guilty of a crime before the crime has been committed.

   As mentioned in Chapter 1, philosophy raises fundamental questions about human life. The author's topic is clearly a philosophical one since it is about our intuitions of right and wrong. In Chapter 5, we learnt the branches of philosophy, so the main topic (at this point in this article) seems to be an ethical one.

2. b. In Chapter 24, we discussed paraphrasing philosophical texts. It seems that Answer b most accurately paraphrases the thesis without relying on the author's own text. Answer a is too close to the original, while Answer c is not as accurate as the other answers.

3. I don't think that either of them can really know what will happen in the future. Algy might think he is going to speed, but perhaps he might change his mind when the time comes. It is also possible that Algy dies suddenly or has an accident that prevents him from being able to drive. Also, Ben cannot really know what Algy will do, since there is no way for Ben to know that Algy is not lying. As mentioned in Chapter 13, claims ought to be clear, consistent, compelling and supported by good arguments. The author's claim that Ben and Algy 'know' that Algy will speed is clear and consistent, but it does not seem to be compelling, nor supported by a good argument. It fails to be compelling for the reasons stated above. Given that a good argument requires true claims as support, we can say that his argument is also not a good one.

4. Epistemology. Although the author's main question about prepunishment is an ethical one, epistemology also plays a role in this article.

5. The example, according to the author, is supposed to 'undermine' the intuition that it is wrong to punish a person before he commits a crime. I am not sure yet whether the example actually shows what it is supposed to show. If we accept his claim that Ben and Algy really do 'know' that Algy will commit the crime, then the author might be right. However, at this point, I am not really sure what to think. He has given me a good reason to question my intuition. I need to read the rest of the argument before giving a final answer to this question. Chapter 11 focused on the importance of counterfactual thinking in philosophical argument. Here, the author is clearly raising a counterfactual question for the reader to think about.

6. I believe the argument is valid, but not sound. As mentioned in Chapter 16, a valid argument is one in which the conclusion necessarily follows from the premises. In this case, if the premise is true, the conclusion must also be true. A sound argument is a valid argument with true premises. In this case, I do not think the premise is true because New clearly described his example as one of prepunishment, not postpunishment.

7. As I said in the answer to Question 3, there are reasons to suppose that Algy might not speed. I think the same reasons hold here and that we do have good reason to doubt that Algy will speed.

8. Although it might look like an appeal to ignorance fallacy, I believe that New is not guilty of committing this fallacy. In Chapter 18, we pointed out that an argument suffers from *ad ignorantium* (appeal to ignorance) when, instead of providing evidence in favour of a position, an arguer supports her own position by merely showing that the position has not been proven wrong. Although the author supports his view that it is coherent that a person might have 'knowledge' (as he defines it) of a crime before it is committed by appealing to the fact that no argument shows it is incoherent, his conclusion is that we are 'provisionally justified' in holding this view. If, on the other hand, he concluded, 'my view is true', then I believe he would have committed a fallacy.

9. In the following sentence, one may find both a descriptive and a normative claim: 'Nevertheless, retributivists may maintain, we all hold, or should hold, the principle that it is wrong to punish an innocent person'. That we all hold such a principle is a descriptive claim, while that we all should hold such a principle is a normative claim. As you learnt in Chapter 12, a descriptive claim describes what is the case and a normative claim states what ought to be the case.

10. I think the following sentence best captures the main idea of the paragraph: 'All that is required is that everyone involved should know the punished person deserves the penalty; and in this case surely that condition is satisfied'. In Chapter 26 we came across suggestions for using quotations effectively. Being able to identify a key sentence or two from each paragraph helps with picking quotations for possible use in an essay.

11. In commercial transactions, we may either pay for purchased items in advance or after receiving the items. In both cases, the author says, the buyer has the obligation to pay. The transaction is analogized to prepunishment by saying that an offender is obligated to 'pay' the penalty, but there is no good reason to assume that the 'payment' must come after the crime has been committed. To evaluate the analogy (see Chapter 17), we must determine whether a commercial transaction is relevantly similar to the payment of a penalty by a criminal. As I see it, the analogy is suspect because a criminal is not purchasing a good in a legal transaction, but is being punished by means of a fine. Algy, in other words, would not be 'buying' anything, thus the obligations on the part of Algy and Ben would not necessarily be the same as the obligations on the part of a buyer and seller.

12. It means 'in accordance with or following from the hypothesis stated'. As mentioned in Chapter 6, it is important to become familiar with philosophical terminology. Although 'ex hypothesi' is not a specific philosophical term, it is one of many Latin terms that is often used by philosophers.

13. I am not certain whether Algy is relevantly similar to the forecaster. It is the forecaster's job to fulfil his obligation, especially one in which people's safety is at risk. Could we likewise say that criminals have an obligation to inform the police of

potential crimes? I think not. While people might have an obligation to obey the law, I am not sure if people have the obligation to inform others before they commit the crime.

14. A deterrence theorist is someone who believes that the primary justification for punishment is to prevent future crime.

15. New would likely say that this argument is invalid because the conclusion does not follow from the premises. Punishing someone for a specific crime not yet committed might not deter that person from committing that particular crime, but it may deter others or even that person from committing a different offence some other time. Thus, New would probably argue there is a morally legitimate reason, from the perspective of a deterrence theorist, for prepunishment.

16. The counter argument to New's argument could be paraphrased as follows:

    1. A criminal committing a crime is like a buyer purchasing an item.
    2. A buyer who pays for an item in advance has a right to that item at a later time.
    _____
    3. Thus, a criminal who pays a penalty in advance has a right to commit the offence at a later time.
    4. A criminal cannot have such a right.
    _____
    5. A criminal is not like a buyer in this respect.
    _____
    6. Thus, the analogy between criminal and buyer does not really support New's argument for the moral legitimacy of prepunishment.

17. 'It is definitive of an offence that the perpetrator has no right to commit it' is not very compelling to me. I would argue that a person has a right to commit a crime as long as the person understands and accepts that punishment might result from the offence.

18. The author's argument might be paraphrased as follows:

    1. If we know that a person will commit a murder and if we impose the death penalty before the murder is committed, then the person would not commit the murder.

2. If the person would not commit the crime, then we cannot impose the death penalty on him as a form of prepunishment.

---

3. Thus, we cannot impose the death penalty as a form of prepunishment.

19. We should accept the requirement of 'reasonable doubt' for prepunishment since we accept it for postpunishment, even though it might lead to miscarriages of justice.
20. Yes. The author restates his main thesis that there is 'no deeper moral obligation' to prepunishment, while addressing the possible objection that prepunishment is a 'strange notion'.

Part B
1. A good paraphrase of the author's thesis is as follows: the central problem with New's argument is that we can never satisfactorily know the information we would need to know to justify prepunishment. Given that thesis, we can say that the author misses the point of New's argument. New is really offering a thought experiment that asks us to imagine such knowledge (or lack of reasonable doubt) is possible. If a philosopher asks, 'What if such and such is the case?', it is not a good response to say, 'Prove to me it can be the case'. Instead, we should question whether the philosopher's answer to the hypothetical scenario is reasonable and well supported. Also, the discussion about the movie seems to take the essay off the track of the main philosophical issues.
2. Generally, the structure of this paper is good. The author has a clear thesis, a logical order to her paper and sticks to the point. However, her use of language is at times tendentious. Moreover, she does not do a very good job of casting New's argument fairly. Notice also the ineffective use of the quotation in this paragraph. I see no good reason to single out the particular phrase 'the conditions of Wilderness One, Algy's car' (see Chapter 26).
3. The author claims that Algy is a criminal with a suspicious character and therefore cannot be trusted to tell the truth.

Yet, according to the hypothetical scenario, Ben must believe Algy in order to punish him legitimately. The author's claim, as an argument against New, is not very compelling. Even if a criminal cannot be trusted to tell the truth, it does not matter because New is asking us to accept his hypothetical scenario in order to make his point about prepunishment. If, for example, I say, 'Imagine that you are a police officer in Mexico and that you do X when Y happens. It follows from this that Z'. If you respond, 'I will never be a police officer in Mexico, so Z cannot follow from your scenario', you are missing the main point of my argument. It is important to note here, as well, that the author does not clearly state what the contradiction is, but relies on the reader to do the hard work of figuring it out. If you think a contradiction exists in an argument, you should clearly spell it out to the reader. This is useful in two respects. First, making such a point clearly is a forceful way to make your argument. Second, and more importantly, if the author had been clearer, she could have potentially realized she was missing the point of New's argument.

4. Neither the style nor integration of the movie is done very well. The essay author assumes background knowledge on the part of the readers that may not exist. Without such background knowledge, a reader would have a difficult time understanding this essay. Beyond this, there is some irony at work in the author's use of the movie in her argument. Her main claim against New is that his counterfactual is not believable, yet she tries to refute him by appealing to a counterfactual herself. *Minority Report* is not a documentary, so it is not very effective to cite one fictional scenario as an argument against the use of another one, especially if your main argument is that the original hypothetical scenario is not believable.

5. The conclusion of Essay 1 is moderately effective insofar as it restates the author's main point and acknowledges the weaknesses of the argument. In this way the conclusion reinforces the impression that the structure of the essay is quite good. Essay 1 is an example of an organized essay but one that does not present an effective philosophical argument.

Part C

1. A good paraphrase of the author's thesis is that prepunishment is morally problematic even if New's counterfactual situation were true. Given this thesis, we can say that she is focusing on relevant philosophical issues in response to the prompt. According to the author, the central problem with New's argument is that prepunishment necessarily involves punishing the innocent.

2. Yes, the author has described the relevant ideas from New's article. She explained the hypothetical scenario, pointed out why the scenario is important and briefly described New's responses to some of the possible objections. The description is objective, generally accurate and quite clear.

3. A paraphrase of the author's argument could go as follows: New's argument relies on a questionable assumption. New's scenario requires us to accept the philosophical view of determinism. This assumption is questionable because an acceptance of determinism means that Algy should not be blamed (because he is 'forced' to act the way he does by prior causes). The author's point is a good one because it focuses on a epistemological and moral issue, namely free will, or whether we can know what we will do and whether we can change our mind about what we will do. Although the author does not make a terribly strong argument to show how New's argument depends on determinism, her discussion of the effect on his argument is well argued. This level of philosophical sophistication is about what we expect from an introductory level philosophy student.

4. The main claim of this paragraph is: 'A portion of New's argument rests on a faulty analogy, which results in rendering the important moral concept of innocence as merely instrumentally valuable'. Here, the author focuses on an important philosophical concept: the moral category of innocence. The author makes a nice move by evaluating the analogy that New makes between legal and illegal transactions and shows that comparing them is illegitimate.

5. The conclusion is effective in three ways: (1) it is respectful of New's argument; (2) it recounts the main points of the author's own argument; (3) and it does not overstate the strength of her own argument leaving the question of determinism and our

doubts on whether our intuitions are correct open to further analysis.

Part D

1. The argument could be put into standard form as follows:

   1. New's argument in 'Time and punishment' claims that if we have knowledge of the future events of a crime, then 'prepunishment' is morally permissible.
   2. Knowledge of future events of a given crime is *improbable* given the nature of the world.
      a. Circumstances surrounding these events usually change.
      b. This knowledge requires us to trust criminals to tell the truth.
   3. Knowledge of future events of a given crime is *impossible* given the fact that human beings have freedom of choice.
   4. Thus, we will never have knowledge of the future events of a crime.

   ---

   5. Therefore, 'prepunishment' is never morally justified.

2. The author of Essay 2 has three arguments against New. The first is a metaphysical and moral one that can be put into standard form as follows:

   1. 'Prepunishment' depends upon determinism.
   2. If determinism is true, then a criminal could not change his mind.
   3. Our intuition is that a criminal could change his mind.

   ---

   4. Therefore, determinism is probably not true.

   ---

   5. Therefore, 'prepunishment' is never morally justified.

The second argument could be put into standard form as follows:

   1. New's argument for 'prepunishment' rests on an analogy between legitimate financial transactions and criminal acts.
   2. Arguments by analogy require analogs that are relevantly similar in order to be convincing.

3. New's analogs, legitimate financial transactions and criminal acts, are not relevantly similar.

---

4. Therefore, New's argument for 'prepunishment' based on this analogy is wrong.

The third argument follows this form:

1. Innocence is an intrinsically valuable moral concept.
2. New's argument for 'prepunishment' fails to treat innocence as instrumental to the concept of justice.

---

3. Thus, New's argument for 'prepunishment' is wrong.

3. Essay 2 does a better job of understanding New's counterfactual situation and the role that it plays in his argument. The purpose of New's hypothetical scenario is to present a story that will allow us to consider the moral issues concerning prepunishment. We can paraphrase the form of his argument as follows: 'If my story is accepted as true, then there is nothing wrong with prepunishment. The only thing preventing us from accepting my story as true are epistemological considerations. Thus, for the purposes of moral argument, my story shows there is nothing *morally wrong* with prepunishment'. The author of Essay 1 is taking issue with the form of New's argument rather than the content by claiming that Ben cannot know that Algy is going to speed. This, however, misses the point of New's counterfactual situation. A second problem with the way in which Essay 1 deals with the counterfactual is that the intuitive strength of the author's objections actually make New's argument stronger. That is, by focusing on the importance of the assumed foreknowledge of Algy's behaviour the author of Essay 1 demonstrates New's basic claim that there is no moral problem with prepunishment.

4. We believe Essay 2 better identifies the correct philosophical issue at stake because it focuses on moral issues, rather than epistemic ones. In other words, the author of Essay 2 focuses on what is right or wrong about prepunishment. As you learnt in Chapter 5, morality is the investigation of issues surrounding

right and wrong, while epistemology studies issues concerning what we can know and how we know it. New's article clearly reveals a moral focus when he states in his first paragraph: 'If this example is valid, it suggests that there may be room in our moral thought for the notion of prepunishment, and that it may be only epistemic, rather than moral, constraints that prevent us from practising it'. Essay 2 maintains this focus on the moral issue and offers arguments against New's conclusion on moral grounds. Essay 1, on the other hand, objects to New's conclusion on epistemic grounds by claiming that we cannot know future states of affairs.

5. Recall from Chapter 17 that informal fallacies are common, seductive types of poor reasoning that we should look to avoid when doing philosophy. While both essays avoid fallacies, Essay 1, at times, borders on an *ad hominem* argument against New. For example, when the student writes 'New also claims, fantastically I might add' she might be intending to convey an opinion of New, as a person, and not of the argument. The tone of the paper is not appropriate since it sometimes borders on criticizing New himself rather than New's arguments.

6. Having answered Questions 1–5 above, it should be clear that the author of Essay 2 better understands the thrust of New's argument. By understanding the role of the counterfactual scenario in New's argument, the author of Essay 2 correctly identifies New's claim that our objections to prepunishment are not moral. Building on this, the author formulates an argument that takes New to task on his moral claim, not the epistemic stipulations in the counterfactual scenario. The author of Essay 1 gets off on the wrong track by failing to see New's central claim as a moral one. The author then develops an argument centered on refuting the epistemic stipulations that New makes. The subsequent argument is not completely bad, but because it starts by misunderstanding New's central claim it fails to answer the question raised by the prompt.

7. In Chapter 25 you learnt two criteria for using quotations effectively. The author of Essay 2 does a much better job of using quotations. She uses five quotations, each of which is relevant. The author of Essay 1, however, used only 1 quotation (in the first paragraph) and the quoted passage was not very powerful.

8. In Chapter 26 you learnt that there are two primary objectives for the introduction of a philosophy paper: (1) offering a clear thesis statement that helps focus the essay by stating a specific and clearly defined philosophical claim; and (2) providing contextual information for a proper appreciation of the philosophical issue you are investigating. In our opinion the author of Essay 2 does this more effectively. The introduction of Essay 2 has a clear thesis with a philosophical claim to argue. It also provides enough contextual information for the reader. By contrast, Essay 1 opens with a rhetorical question: 'How can we know what a person will do tomorrow'? This is not the most effective way to begin an argument. Additionally, the introduction of Essay 2 provides a 'roadmap' for the reader to follow. Essay 1 contains contextual information, but in some ways fails to help the reader anticipate the structure of the argument that follows.

Also in Chapter 26, you learnt that the conclusion of a philosophy paper should reinforce and close your argument by doing two things: (1) restating the main evidence and inferences that support your thesis; and (2) acknowledging possible weaknesses in your argument or possible avenues for future investigation. The author of Essay 1 does restate her main claim in the conclusion. She also recapitulates some of her main points against New's argument: 'Algy can blow a tire, Alaska could suffer an earth quake, or the Wilderness One highway could be closed tomorrow. . . .Why should we trust Algy, or anyone else? People lie all the time and Algy could be lying now'. However, the author of Essay 2 does a far better job of concluding her essay. She includes a thumbnail sketch of arguments and acknowledges the fact that there are important unanswered questions that remain on the subject of prepunishment, thereby not overstating the strength of her own argument.

9. We think that Essay 2 presents its argument in a much clearer way. The author of Essay 1 often deviates from her thesis making it difficult for the reader to follow her argument. The author of Essay 2 argues that New's claim that there is no moral argument against prepunishment is incorrect. The author of Essay 2 keeps her main point, namely that there is still a moral problem regarding punishment of the innocent, in view throughout

the essay without deviating. She reiterates this point regularly, keeping the reader informed of her thesis and how her points relate to it. While clarity is important, it is not the most important criterion for judgment. Clarity makes it easier to see and understand an argument; it does not make an argument good.

10. In our opinion, Essay 2 does a better job at the relevant tasks of doing philosophy. It more accurately and fully describes New's argument, it focuses more on the relevant issues, it uses better quotations and it offers a decent critical evaluation of New's argument.

Notes

Chapter 1

1 French, P. (2004), *Ethics of College Sports*. New York: Rowman and Littlefield, p. 110.
2 Reiman, J. (2004), *Rich Get Richer*. Boston: Pearson, pp. 84–85.
3 *NY Times* (2010), Editorial, June 8.

Chapter 2

1 Nilson, L. (2010), *Teaching at Its Best*. San Francisco: Jossey-Bass, p. 215.
2 Minton, A. and Shipka, T. (1996), *Philosophy: Paradox and Discovery*. New York: McGraw Hill, p. 191.
3 Taylor, R. (1992), *Metaphysics*. Englewood Cliffs, NJ: Prentice Hall, p. 58.
4 Rachels, J. (1986), *The Elements of Moral Philosophy*. New York: Random House, p. 14.
5 Camus, A. (1991), *The Myth of Sissyphus*. New York: Vintage International, pp. 3–4.
6 Rahula, W. (1975), *What the Buddha Taught*. New York: Grove Press, pp. 21–2.

Chapter 3

1 Nilson, L. (2010), *Teaching at Its Best*. San Francisco: Jossey-Bass, pp. 123–4.
2 Plato. (2008), *Euthyphro*, trans. B. Jowett, retrieved from the *Project Gutenberg Ebook*, webpage,www.gutenberg.org/files/1642/1642-h/1642-h.htm.

Chapter 4

1 Bean, J., Ramage, J. and Johnson, J. (2006), *The Alleyn & Bacon Guide to Writing*. New York: Pearson, p. 42.

Chapter 6

1 D'Holbach, B. (1770), 'Of the system of man's free agency' in *The System of Nature*. Quoted from Pojman, L. (2006), *Philosophy: The Quest for Truth*. Oxford: Oxford University Press, p. 350.

2 Stace, W. T. (1952), *Religion and the Modern Mind*. Philadelphia: J.B. Lippincott, p. 257.

3 Descartes, R. (1993), *Meditations on First Philosophy*, trans. D. A. Cress. Indianapolis: Hackett, p. 51.

4 Ryle, G. (1949), *The Concept of Mind*. New York: Barnes and Noble, p. 22.

5 Fodor, J. (1981), 'The mind–body problem', *Scientific American*, 244(1), p. 118.

6 Berkeley, G. (1979), *Three Dialogues between Hylas and Philonous*. Indianapolis: Hackett, p. 94.

7 Hobbes, T. (1968), *Leviathan*. London: Penguin, p. 428.

Chapter 7

1 Kant, I. (1965), *Critique of Pure Reason*, trans. N. K. Smith. New York: St. Martin's Press, p. 41.

2 Locke, J. (1975), *An Essay Concerning Human Understanding*. Oxford: Clarendon Press, p. 104.

3 Plato. (2002), 'Phaedo' in *Five Dialogues*. Indianapolis: Hackett, p. 102.

4 Russell, B. (1968), *The Analysis of Mind*. London: George Allen & Unwin, p. 159.

5 Hume, D. (1988), *An Enquiry Concerning Human Understanding*. Amherst, NY: Prometheus Books, p. 21.

6 Descartes, R. (1993), *Meditations on First Philosophy*, trans. D. A. Cross. Indianapolis: Hackett, p. 34.

7 Locke, J. (1975), *An Essay Concerning Human Understanding*. Oxford: Clarendon, p. 137.

8 Russell, B. (1912), *The Problems of Philosophy*. Oxford: Oxford University Press, p. 130.

9 Bradley, F.H. (1914), *Essays on Truth and Reality*. Oxford: Oxford University Press, p. 210.

10 James, W. (1991), *Pragmatism*. Buffalo: Prometheus Books, p. 88.

Chapter 8

1 Rand, A. (1964), *The Virtue of Selfishness*. New York: New American Library, p. 44.

2 Benedict, R. (1934), 'Anthropology and the Abnormal', *Journal of General Psychology*, 10, 73.

3 Kant, I. (1949), *Fundamental Principles of the Metaphysic of Morals*, trans. T. Abbott. Indianapolis: Bobbs-Merrill, p. 18.

4 Aristotle (1999), *Nicomachean Ethics*, trans. T. Irwin. Indianapolis: Hackett, p. 19.

5 Mill, J.S. (2001), *Utilitarianism*. Indianapolis: Hackett, p. 7.

6 Ibid., p. 35.

7 Bentham, J. (1970), *An Introduction to the Principles of Morals and Legislation*. Oxford: Oxford University Press, p. 11.

Chapter 9

1 Locke, J. (1980), *Second Treatise of Government*. Indianapolis: Hackett, p. 52.

2 Plato (1992), *The Republic*, trans. G. M. A. Grube and C. D. C. Reeve. Indianapolis: Hackett, p. 148.

3 Marx, K. (1964), *The Economic and Philosophic Manuscripts of 1844*. New York: International Publishers, p. 139.

4 Nozick, R. (1974), *Anarchy, State, and Utopia*. New York: Basic Books, p. ix.

5 Hobbes, T. (1969), *The Elements of Law: Natural and Politic*. London: Frank Cass and Co., p. 103.

6 Tocqueville, A. (1947), *Democracy in America*. Oxford: Oxford University Press, p. 162.

7 Machiavelli, N. (1961), *The Prince*. New York: Penguin, pp. 99–100.

8 Rawls, J. (1971), *A Theory of Justice*. Cambridge: Harvard University Press, p. 60.

Chapter 10

1 Russell, B. (1961), *Religion and Science*. Oxford: Oxford University Press, p. 243.

2 Spinoza, B. (2000), *Ethics*, trans. G. H. R. Parkinson. Oxford: Oxford University Press, p. 93.

3 Aquinas, T. (1954), *Nature and Grace: Selections from the Summa Theologica of Thomas Aquinas*, trans. A. M. Fairweather. Philadelphia: Westminster Press, p. 54.

4 Ibid., p. 56.

5 Augustine. (1993), *On Free Choice of the Will*. Indianapolis: Hackett, p. 82.

6 Kierkegaard, S. (1941), *Concluding Unscientific Postscript*, trans. D. Swenson and W. Lowrie. Princeton: Princeton University Press, p. 189.

Chapter 11

1 Locke, J. (1975), *An Essay Concerning Human Understanding*. Oxford: Clarendon Press, p. 238.
2 Nozick, R. (1974), *Anarchy, State, and Utopia*. New York: Basic Books, p. 42.
3 Pascal, B. (1965), *Pensees*, trans. H. F. Stewart. New York: Pantheon Books, p. 117.
4 Thomson, J. J. (1971), 'A defense of abortion', *Philosophy and Public Affairs*, 1(1), p. 59.
5 Perry, J. (1972), 'Can the self divide?', *Journal of Philosophy*, 69(16), p. 463.

Chapter 13

1 Plato (2002), *Five Dialogues*. Indianapolis: Hackett, pp. 34 and 43.
2 Machiavelli, N. (1982), *The Prince*, trans. G. Bull. Middlesex: Penguin, pp. 90–1.
3 Nietzsche, F. (1968), *The Will to Power*, trans. W. Kaufmann and R. J. Hollingdale. New York: Vintage, p. 298.
4 Sartre, J. (1957), *Existentialism and Human Emotions*. New York: Wisdom Library, pp. 17–18.
5 Heidegger, M. (1977), 'Letter on humanism' in *Basic Writings*, trans. F. A. Capuzzi and J. G. Gray. New York: Harper and Row, p. 193.

Chapter 17

1 Aristotle (1984), *The Complete Works of Aristotle*, ed. Jonathan Barnes, Vol. 2. Princeton: Princeton University Press, p. 1743.
2 Stephen, J. F. (1967), *Liberty Equality, Fraternity*. Cambridge: Cambridge University Press, p. 85.
3 Nozick, R. (1974), *Anarchy, State, and Utopia*. New York: Basic Books, p. 263.
4 Mill, J. S. (2010), *Utilitarianism*, ed. John Bennet. www.earlymoderntexts.com, p. 24.
5 Walzer, M. (2006), *Just and Unjust Wars: A Moral Argument with Historical Illustrations*. New York: Basic Books, pp. 58–9.
6 Hume, D. (1993), *The Natural History of Religion*, ed. J. A. C. Gaskin. Oxford and New York: Oxford University Press, p. 45.

Chapter 19

1 Rousseau, J. (1979), *Emile or On Education*, trans. H. Bloom. New York: Basic Books, p. 48.

2 Popper, K. (1974), *Conjectures and Refutations: The Growth of Scientific Knowledge*. London: Routledge and Kegan Paul, p. 216.

3 Kant, I. (1949), *Fundamental Principles of the Metaphysic of Morals*, trans. T. K. Abbott. Indianapolis: Bobbs-Merrill, p. 11.

4 Descartes, R., *Meditations on First Philosophy*, trans. D. A. Cross. Indianapolis: Hackett.

5 Hick, J. (1983), *Philosophy of Religion*. Englewood Cliffs, NJ: Prentice-Hall, pp. 40–1.

Chapter 20

1 Hobbes, T. (1968), *Leviathan*. London: Penguin, pp. 363–4.

Chapter 21

1 Bean, J., Ramage, J. and Johnson, J. (2006), *The Alleyn & Bacon Guide to Writing*. New York: Pearson, p. 11.

Chapter 23

1 Van den Haag, E. (1986), 'The ultimate punishment: A defense', *Harvard Law Review*, 99(7), pp. 1664–5.

Chapter 24

1 Gay-Williams, J. (1992), 'The wrongfulness of euthanasia', *Intervention and Reflection: Basic Issues in Medical Ethics*, ed. R. Munson. Belmont, CA: Wadsworth, p. 169.

2 Ibid.

3 Ibid.

4 Ibid.

5 Hume, D. (1988), *An Enquiry Concerning Human Understanding*. Amherst, NY: Prometheus Books, p. 75.

6 Hobbes, T. (1968), *Leviathan*. London: Penguin, p. 263.

7 Antiphon, 'Fragment' in *A Presocratics Reader,* ed. P. Curd, trans. R. McKirahan. Indianapolis: Hackett, p. 107.

8 Kant, I. (1970), *Kant's Political Writings*, trans. H. S. Nisbet. Cambridge: Cambridge University Press, p. 47.
9 Mackie, J. L. (1982), *The Miracle of Theism: Arguments for and against the Existence of God*. Oxford: Clarendon Press, p. 175.

Chapter 25

1 Gay-Williams, J. (1992), 'The wrongfulness of euthanasia', Intervention and Reflection: Basic Issues in Medical Ethics, edited by R. Munson. Belmont, CA: Wadsworth, p. 169.

Chapter 26

1 Thomson, J. J. (1971), 'A defense of abortion', *Philosophy and Public Affairs*, 1, p. 52.
2 Rorty, R. (1998), *Achieving Our Country*. Cambridge: Harvard University Press, p. 75.

Chapter 28

1 Bean, J., Ramage, J. and Johnson, J. (2006), *The Alleyn & Bacon Guide to Writing*. New York: Pearson, pp. 519–20.

Chapter 30

1 New, C. (1992), 'Time and punishment,' *Analysis*, 52(1), pp. 35–40. Reprinted with permission of the Oxford University Press.
2 Ibid., p. 35.
3 Ibid., p. 36.
4 Ibid., p. 37.
5 Ibid., p. 37.

Glossary

A posteriori Claim: A claim that seems true or false by virtue of experience.

A priori Claim: A claim that seems to be true by virtue of its terms, that is, either by definition or by the relation of its terms to each other.

Absolutism: The political doctrine and practice of an unlimited sovereign authority to which citizens are absolutely obliged and whose power is not regulated by another authority.

Ad hominem: An argument that is faulty because it criticizes the person making an argument rather than a position or argument.

Ad ignorantium (appeal to ignorance): An argument that is faulty because instead of providing evidence in favour of a position, it merely shows that the position has not been proven wrong.

Ad populum (appeal to general belief): An argument that is faulty because it provides evidence for the truth of a conclusion based only on the general appeal of the belief.

Ad verecundiam (appeal to inappropriate authority): An argument that is faulty because it makes a claim based on the testimony of a person unqualified to provide expert knowledge on the given subject.

Agnosticism: The claim that we cannot know whether God exists or not due to lack of evidence.

Altruism: The view that selfless acts are possible.

Anarchism: The view that the state ought to be abolished because it is unnecessary, undesirable and/or harmful.

Argument: A series of claims in which one of the claims (i.e., the conclusion) is said to follow from, or be supported by, one or more of the other claims (i.e., the premises).

Aristocracy: A form of government in which those deemed the 'best' rule.

Atheism: The claim that God does not exist.

Claim: An assertion that something either is, or ought to be, the case.

Classical Liberalism: A political doctrine that emphasizes the rights and freedoms of individuals and therefore promotes a limited government.

Cogent Argument: An inductive argument that makes a strong case for the truth of the conclusion on the basis of true premises.

Coherence Theory of Truth: The theory that statements are true or false insofar as they cohere with a body of accepted propositions.

Compatibilism (or Soft Determinism): The dual assertion that (i) our actions are necessarily and causally determined and (ii) that we are nevertheless to be held morally responsible for at least some of our actions.

Conclusion: The claim in an argument that is, or is meant to be, supported by the other claims (premises).

Consequentialism: Any ethical theory that evaluates the morality of an act on the basis of the act's consequences.

Constructivism: The theory that knowledge is constructed by the mind out of data given by sense experience.

Conventional Ethical Relativism: A form of ethical relativism that asserts that ethical standards are determined by the collective beliefs of a particular society.

Correspondence Theory of Truth: The theory that statements are true or false insofar as they represent the objective aspects of reality.

Cosmological Argument: An argument that attempts to prove that God exists from an alleged fact (or facts) about the world.

Counterfactual Situation (or thought experiment): A hypothetical or imaginary scenario often beginning with the question, 'What if?'

Deductive Argument: An argument in which the conclusion is supposed to follow from the premises necessarily. This does not guarantee that the premises are true, rather if they are, then the conclusion must follow.

Democracy: A form of government in which the people rule, either directly by themselves or indirectly through a system of elected representatives.

Deontological Ethics: Any ethical theory that evaluates the morality of an act on the basis of the morality of the act itself.

Descriptive Claim: A claim that describes that something is the case. Often opposed to a normative claim that claims something ought to be the case.

Design Argument: An argument that attempts to prove that God exists from the perceived order or purpose in nature.

Determinism: The assertion that every event is the necessary consequence of prior causes.

Distributive Justice: A form of justice related to the distribution of goods among members of a commonwealth.

Eliminativism: A form of physicalism that denies the existence of a non-physical mind and also jettisons language that refers to the mind.

Empiricism: The view that the primary source of our knowledge of reality is our sense experience.

Enthymeme: An argument in which one of the claims is not explicitly stated.

Epistemology: The branch of philosophy that is concerned with the possibility, sources and conditions of knowledge. It raises such questions as: How do you know what you know? What is the difference between opinion and knowledge?

Ethical Egoism: The theory that individuals ought to act to promote their own interests.

Ethical Hedonism: A form of ethical egoism that says humans should act to promote their own pleasure.

Ethical Objectivism: The view that universal and objective ethical standards do exist.

Ethical Relativism: The view that no universal and objective ethical standards exist, but that all moral judgments are a matter of opinion.

Ethics: The branch of philosophy that poses questions about the nature of morality and how we ought to behave. It asks such questions as: Are moral standards absolute or relative? What makes an action morally praiseworthy? Is a given human practice, such as the death penalty or abortion, moral or immoral?

Evidentialism: The claim that objective evidence is required to support one's belief in God.

Fallacy: An argument that contains an error in reasoning.

False Dilemma: An argument that is faulty because it stipulates that only two alternatives exist in a given situation when, in reality, there are more possibilities.

Fideism: The claim that faith alone justifies one's belief in God.

Functionalism: The view that the mental states are constituted by the functional role they play.

Hard Determinism: The dual assertion that (i) a free will is necessary for people to be held morally responsible for their actions and that (ii) people do not have free will.

Hasty Generalization: An argument that is faulty because the support for the conclusion is based on generalizations derived from insufficient data.

Idealism: A form of metaphysical monism that holds that reality is entirely mental or spiritual in nature.

Identity Theory (or Reductionism): A form of physicalism asserting that claims about the mind can be reduced to claims about brain states.

Incompatibilism: The assertion that determinism is not compatible with the kind of freedom necessary for the moral evaluation of our actions.

Inductive Argument: An argument in which the conclusion is intended to follow probably from the premises.

Infer: The act of determining that a conclusion follows logically from the premises.

Innate Ideas: Inborn ideas that we have prior to any experience.

Instrumental Value: The ethical or philosophical value that something has because of the ends that may be achieved by means of it.

Interactionism: A form of mind-body dualism asserting that the mind and body interact with each other even though they are distinct entities.

Intrinsic Value: The ethical or philosophical value that something has 'in itself'.

Libertarianism: The view that human choices are not causally determined by prior events, but are free.

Logic: The branch of philosophy concerned with evaluating philosophical arguments. Logicians ask such questions as: What is a good argument? How do I recognize a bad argument? What are the elements of good philosophical thinking?

Materialism: A form of metaphysical monism asserting that reality consists of only material entities.

Meritocracy: A form of government in which rulers are chosen based upon demonstrated talent and ability.

Metaphysical Dualism: The position that reality consists of two kinds of substances.

Metaphysical Monism: The position that reality consists of one kind of substance.

Metaphysics: The branch of philosophy that poses questions about the nature of reality and human existence, such as: What is the nature of reality? What is the relationship between mind and body? Are human decisions determined by prior events and causes, or are they freely made?

Mind–Body Dualism: The assertion that the mind and body are two separate entities.

Monotheism: The belief that only one God exists.

Nonevidentialism: The claim that our fundamental beliefs about life do not require rational justification.

Normative Claim: A claim that prescribes what ought to be the case. Often opposed to descriptive claims that claim something is the case.

Objectivism: The view that there are facts about the world independent of us.

Ontological Argument: An argument that attempts to prove that God exists by use of intuition and reason alone, without relying on any type of empirical evidence.

Pantheism: The belief that God is identical with nature.

Perspectivism: The theory that all facts or truths must be interpreted from one perspective or another.

Petitio Principii (begging the question or circular reasoning): An argument that is faulty because the conclusion of the argument is assumed within one of the premises instead of providing any evidence for the conclusion.

Philosophy of Religion: The branch of philosophy that seeks answers to fundamental questions about religion, God and the afterlife.

It poses such questions as: Does God exist? What is the relationship between faith and reason? Why would an all-loving God allow evil to exist?

Physicalism: The view that everything, including the human self, is physical.

Political Libertarianism: A doctrine that seeks to maximize individual liberty and to minimize, or even abolish, the state.

Political Philosophy: The branch of philosophy that is concerned with the nature, extent and justification of government, as well as the role of the individual in society. Political philosophers pose such questions as: What is the source of political authority? What are the rights and duties of both governments and citizens?

Polytheism: The belief that many gods exist.

Pragmatic Theory of Truth: The theory that the truth of propositions should be accepted to the extent that they are useful.

Premise: A claim used in an argument that provides support for the truth of another claim (i.e., the conclusion).

Primary Qualities: The properties of an object that are possessed independent of any observer.

Primary Text: A text that is meant to be a work of philosophy in and of itself.

Problem of Evil: The problem of trying to explain why God, who is believed to be omnipotent and all powerful, would allow evil to exist.

Psychological Hedonism: A form of psychological egoism that claims all human actions are motivated by a desire to attain pleasure and avoid pain.

Rationalism: The view that the primary source of our knowledge of reality is the faculty of reason.

Reductionism: See Identity Theory.

Retributive Justice: A form of justice concerned with the punishment of crimes.

Scepticism: The view that we cannot have genuine knowledge.

Secondary Qualities: The properties of an object that cause certain subjective sensations in the observer, sensations that do not accurately reflect the object.

Secondary Text: A commentary on a primary text meant to elucidate the arguments and ideas of the primary text.

Social Contract Theory: A theory that justifies the government's authority by reference to an explicit or implicit contract made by the members of a given society.

Socialism: A political and economic theory advocating the common ownership of the means of production and of the distribution of resources.

Soft Determinism: See Compatibilism.

Sound Argument: An argument that follows a valid form and the premises are true.

Standard Form: An argument in standard form is one in which the premises and conclusions are numbered in logical order and the conclusion is separated from the premises by a line.

Straw Man Fallacy: An argument that is faulty because the arguer attacks a weakened or distorted view of the original argument.

Subjective Ethical Relativism: A form of ethical relativism that asserts that ethical standards are determined by each individual's personal beliefs.

Subjectivism: The assertion that truth is relative to each person's individual perspective.

Theism: The claim that at least one deity exists.

Theocracy: A form of government in which a God or a deity (or an official representative of the divine) is recognized as the legitimate ruler.

Theodicy: An attempt to explain why God would allow evil to exist.

Tyrant: A leader who abuses political power to an extreme extent.

Valid Argument: An argument in which the truth of the conclusion necessarily follows from the truth of the premises.

Virtue Ethics: Any ethical theory that emphasizes the character of human beings, rather than rules or consequences.

Bibliography

Antiphon (1996), 'Fragment', in ed. P. Curd, *A Presocratics Reader*, trans. R. McKirahan. Indianapolis: Hackett, pp. 104–5.

Aquinas, T. (1954), *Nature and Grace: Selections from the Summa Theologica of Thomas Aquinas*, trans. A. M. Fairweather. Philadelphia: Westminster Press.

Aristotle (1984), *The Complete Works of Aristotle*, ed. Jonathan Barnes, Vol. 2. Princeton: Princeton University Press.

—. (1999), *Nicomachean Ethics*, trans. T. Irwin. Indianapolis: Hackett.

Augustine (1993), *On Free Choice of the Will*. Indianapolis: Hackett.

Bean, J., Ramage, J. and Johnson, J. (2006), *The Alleyn & Bacon Guide to Writing*. New York: Pearson.

Benedict, R. (1934), 'Anthropology and the Abnormal', *Journal of General Psychology*, 10, pp. 59–82.

Bentham, J. (1970), *An Introduction to the Principles of Morals and Legislation*. Oxford: Oxford University Press, p. 11.

Berkeley, G. (1979), *Three Dialogues Between Hylas and Philonous*, Indianapolis: Hackett.

Blocker, H. G, Petrick, J. and Stewart, D. (2010), *The Fundamentals of Philosophy*. Boston: Prentice Hall.

Bradley, F. H. (1914), *Essays on Truth and Reality*. Oxford: Oxford University Press.

Camus, A. (1991), *The Myth of Sisyphus*. New York: Vintage International.

Descartes, R. (1993), *Meditations on First Philosophy*, trans. D. A. Cross. Indianapolis: Hackett.

Fodor, J. (1981), 'The Mind–Body Problem', *Scientific American*, 244(1), pp. 124–32.

French, P. (2004), *Ethics of College Sports*. New York: Rowman and Littlefield.

Gay-Williams, J. (1992), 'The Wrongfulness of Euthanasia', in ed. R. Munson, *Intervention and Reflection: Basic Issues in Medical Ethics*. Belmont, CA: Wadsworth, pp. 168–71.

Heidegger, M. (1977), 'Letter on Humanism', in *Basic Writings*, trans. F. A. Capuzzi and J. G. Gray. New York: Harper and Row.

Hick, J. (1983), *Philosophy of Religion*. Englewood Cliffs, NJ: Prentice-Hall, pp. 40–1.

Hobbes, T. (1968), *Leviathan*. London: Penguin.

—. (1969), *The Elements of Law: Natural and Politic*. London: Frank Cass and Co.

Hume, D. (1988), *An Enquiry Concerning Human Understanding*. Amherst, NY: Prometheus Books.

—. (1993), *The Natural History of Religion*, ed. J. A. C. Gaskin. Oxford and New York: Oxford University Press.

James, W. (1991), *Pragmatism*. Buffalo: Prometheus Books.

Kant, I. (1949), *Fundamental Principles of the Metaphysic of Morals*, trans. T. Abbott. Indianapolis: Bobbs-Merrill.

—. (1965), *Critique of Pure Reason*, trans. N. K. Smith. New York: St. Martin's Press.

—. (1970), *Kant's Political Writings*, trans. H. S. Nisbet. Cambridge: Cambridge University Press.

Kierkegaard, S. (1941), *Concluding Unscientific Postscript*, trans. D. Swenson and W. Lowrie. Princeton: Princeton University Press.

Locke, J. (1975), *An Essay Concerning Human Understanding*. Oxford: Clarendon Press.

—. (1980), *Second Treatise of Government*. Indianapolis: Hackett.

Machiavelli, N. (1982), *The Prince*, trans. G. Bull. Middlesex: Penguin.

Mackie, J. L. (1982), *The Miracle of Theism: Arguments for and Against the Existence of God*. Oxford: Clarendon Press.

Marx, K. (1964), *The Economic and Philosophic Manuscripts of 1844*. New York: International Publishers.

Mill, J. S. (2001), *Utilitarianism*. Indianapolis: Hackett.

Minton, A. and Shipka, T. (1996), *Philosophy: Paradox and Discovery*. New York: McGraw Hill.

New, C. (1992), 'Time and Punishment', *Analysis*, 52(1), pp. 35–40.

Nietzsche, F. (1968), *The Will to Power*, trans. W. Kaufmann and R. J. Hollingdale. New York: Vintage.

Nilson, L. (2010), *Teaching at Its Best*. San Francisco: Jossey-Bass.

Nozick, R. (1974), *Anarchy, State, and Utopia*. New York: Basic Books.

NY Times (2010), 'The Digital Pulse', Editorial, 8 June.

Pascal, B. (1965), *Pensees*, trans. H. F. Stewart. New York: Pantheon Books.

Perry, J. (1972), 'Can the Self Divide?', *Journal of Philosophy*, 69(16), pp. 463–88.

Plato (1992), *The Republic*, trans. G. M. A. Grube and C. D. C. Reeve. Indianapolis: Hackett.

—. (2002), *Five Dialogues*. Indianapolis: Hackett.

—. (2008), *Euthyphro*, trans. B. Jowett, retrieved from the Project Gutenberg Ebook webpage,www.gutenberg.org/files/1642/1642-h/1642-h.htm.

Pojman, L. (2006), *Philosophy: The Quest for Truth*. Oxford: Oxford University Press.

Rachels, J. (1986), *The Elements of Moral Philosophy*. New York: Random House.

Rahula, W. (1975), *What the Buddha Taught*. New York: Grove Press.

Rand, A. (1964), *The Virtue of Selfishness*. New York: New American Library.

Rawls, J. (1971), *A Theory of Justice*. Cambridge: Harvard University Press.

Reiman, J. (2004), *Rich Get Richer*. Boston: Pearson.

Rorty, R. (1998), *Achieving Our Country*. Cambridge: Harvard University Press.

Rousseau, J. (1979), *Emile or On Education*, trans. H. Bloom. New York: Basic Books.

Russell, B. (1912), *The Problems of Philosophy*. Oxford: Oxford University Press.

—. (1961), *Religion and Science*. Oxford: Oxford University Press.

—. (1968), *The Analysis of Mind*. London: George Allen & Unwin.

Ryle, G. (1949), *The Concept of Mind*. New York: Barnes and Noble.

Sartre, J. (1957), *Existentialism and Human Emotions*. New York: Wisdom Library.

Spinoza, B. (2000), *Ethics*, trans. G. H. R. Parkinson. Oxford: Oxford University Press.

Stace, W. T. (1952), *Religion and the Modern Mind*. Philadelphia: J. B. Lippincott.

Stephen, J. F. (1967), *Liberty Equality, Fraternity*. Cambridge: Cambridge University Press.

Tarski, A. (1944), 'The Semantic Conception of Truth and the Foundations of Semantics', *Philosophy and Phenomenological Research*, 4(3), pp. 341–76.

Taylor, R. (1992), *Metaphysics*. Englewood Cliffs, NJ: Prentice Hall.

Thomson, J. J. (1971), 'A Defense of Abortion', *Philosophy and Public Affairs*, 1(1), pp. 46–66.

Tocqueville, A. (1947), *Democracy in America*. Oxford: Oxford University Press.

Van den Haag, E. (1986), 'The Ultimate Punishment: a Defense', *Harvard Law Review*, 99(7), pp. 1662–9.

Walzer, M. (2006), *Just and Unjust Wars: A Moral Argument with Historical Illustrations*. New York: Basic Books.

Index